Sales Greatness

SALES PRINCIPLES FOR
CONSTANT TOP PERFORMANCE
IN MODERN TIMES

* * *

Simon Lightfield

© 2016 by Simon Lightfield

All rights reserved. No part of this book may be reproduced in any written form, electronic form, recording, or photocopying without written permission of the publisher or author. The exception would be in the case of brief quotations in articles, reviews, or web pages.

Although every precaution has been taken to verify the accuracy of the information contained herein, the author and publisher assume no responsibility for any errors or omissions.

www.SellingGreatness.com

ISBN: 1537678124
ISBN 13: 9781537678122

Thank You!

* * *

THANK YOU FOR PRIORITIZING YOUR growth as a sales consultant!

All those who prioritize learning and growing increase their capacity to help the people around them. Sales is all about helping others in various ways, and you are probably already helping other people in a lot of ways. The more you learn, the more you can give to the world.

Contents.

	Introduction.	xi
Chapter 1	The Secret to Consistency in Sales.	1
	To Be Great in Sales, We Need to Have Great Days Every Day.	1
	Be Aware of All the Principles, and Increase Their Power.	2
	Three Simple Rules for Sales Greatness.	3
	How Can You Make Your Sales Success Inevitable?	4
	The Advantages of Being a Great Sales Consultant.	5
Chapter 2	How to Think about Your Product to Sell Effectively.	7
	You Have to Be Interested in What You Sell.	7
	Modern, Elite Sales Consultants Focus on Helping.	10
	Experience Your Product at Its Best!	11
	The Most Effective Mind-Set in Selling.	12
	What Are the Benefits of Becoming the Best Sales Consultant You Can Be?	14
	Are You Going to Become as Great as You Can Be?	15
	Dream Your Natural Dreams.	16
Chapter 3	Realizing Your True Sales Potential.	19
	Human Potential.	19
	PMA.	19
	PMA regarding the Product.	21

	PMA regarding Yourself.	21
	PMA regarding the Transaction.	23
	PMA regarding Your Job.	25
	Think about All the Benefits of Your Product That the Customer Will Enjoy.	27

Chapter 4	Fundamental Energies in Modern Sales.	29
	Life-Force.	29
	Self-Esteem.	31
	The Way You Open.	33
	Flow.	35
	Be Brave, and Get Out of Your Comfort Zone.	37
	Be Natural!	38
	Be Immersed in Your Conversation.	38
	Know That the Customer Is Lucky!	40
	Perfect Authority.	40
	Involvement of the Customer.	40
	Get Them to Agree and Say Yes.	41

Chapter 5	Attitudes and Principles for Greatness in Modern Times.	43
	Standard for Yourself.	43
	Focus.	44
	Read and Acquire Knowledge from Successful Sales Consultants.	45
	Think for Yourself.	48
	Hard Work.	48
	Effectiveness.	51
	Pushing.	52
	How to Handle Objections.	54
	Product Knowledge.	56

Chapter 6	Mind-Sets That Help You Create Your Own Closing Techniques.	58
	Closing.	58

Chapter 7	Simple Keys to Optimize Your Confidence.	68
	Confidence.	68
	Relationship.	70
	Professionalism.	72
	Enthusiasm.	74
	Amplify Emotions.	77
	Needs.	79
	Being Authentic.	82
	Vocal Techniques.	89
Chapter 8	How You Can Shape the Future of Your Sales Career.	93
	Sales Training.	93
	Of Course the Customer Is Receiving Your Product.	96
	Re-Gear.	98
	Efficiency.	101
	Make the Customer Feel Great.	103
	Go the Extra Mile.	104
	Focus on the Positive Things.	105
	Connection.	106
	Guts.	108
Chapter 9	Body Language and Adding Value to Your Product by Being Your Best Self.	110
	Body Language.	110
	Habits.	113
	You Have Much More Power Than You Think!	119
	Recovery.	120
	Sleep.	121
	Put Yourself in the Same State of Mind You Want Your Customers to Be In.	124
	The Science and the Art of Sales.	125
	Say Things in a Way That Helps Customers Understand and Learn Something.	125
	They're Buying the Feeling That You Represent.	126

  Spread Joy. 126
  Happiness. 128
  Celebrating. 129

Chapter 10 Build upon What Works. 131
  Write It Down. 131
  Visualizing. 132
  With Customers on the Line. 134
  Always Agree with the Customer. 135
  No One Knows Anything. 135

Chapter 11 Powerfully Being Yourself. 137
  Be Human. 137
  Identity Is the Most Powerful Driving Force in
  Behavior, Performance, and Results. 138
  You Are in Charge. 140
  Know the Success Factors and Dial Them In. 140
  Imagine That You're Giving This Away for Free. 143
  Toughness. 144
  Caring. 148
  Being Just Good Enough to Close the Sale. 148

Chapter 12 Additional Tips and Strategies. 150
  Race against the Clock. 150
  Keep It Simple. 152
  Working during the Silences. 153
  Every Day Is a New Day. 156

  Summary. 157
  Receive Optimal Tips! 159

Introduction.

* * *

Sales is an ever-evolving field of study. To succeed in new times, we need new skills and new perspectives. Adaptation is one of the most useful skills the highest achievers can master.

Those who are truly great do whatever it takes to acquire and implement new knowledge, and you are one of these people.

The timeless principles, new strategies, insightful mind-sets, and recommendations in this book will allow you to take the next steps toward realizing your personal sales greatness.

To multiply our incomes, be truly great at sales, and realize our dreams, we must implement the same knowledge as those who are already living their dreams. Not only must we acquire the surface-level techniques, but more importantly, we must embody the mind-sets, paradigms, and identities that these high achievers have.

To become an even greater sales consultant, you must also form your own powerful mind-sets if you want to reach an even higher level and surpass your teachers.

In hypnosis and persuasion, we find that repetition is a powerful tool to help people make lasting changes. So if you find that some ideas are repeated in this book, know that this is done on purpose. This will drive the ideas deeper into your subconscious mind and make sure you comprehend more of the information in this book when you have finished it. It is also done to help your subconscious be more inspired to take certain actions.

CHAPTER 1

The Secret to Consistency in Sales.

* * *

To Be Great in Sales, We Need to Have Great Days Every Day.

The key to constant top performance in sales is to be intimately aware of all the necessary principles of sales success.

Some salespeople have great days all the time, while those who are right on the verge of achieving greatness have some good days but can't seem to reach top performance every day.

What is the secret to consistency in sales? First, the greatest sales consultants of all time are truly aware of all the necessary principles for success. If you can clearly see all the principles in front of you as you are selling, then you can adjust how you sell, as you notice what you are doing right and are not doing right. In sales, there are hundreds of principles, and the more of them you know, the better.

Most salespeople have a mix of good days and not so good days. The reason for this is that they don't understand all the necessary principles for sales success and haven't implemented them powerfully enough. Good sales consultants might know eighty of the one hundred principles they need to know. They will practice the principles they know about, but it will be up to chance whether the other, unseen principles will also be implemented. One example is the principle of happiness and smiling; it's one that is fairly simple but sometimes overlooked.

If sales consultants do other principles right, like tailoring the offering to the customer, mirroring the customer, and closing correctly, they may still get the sale. Some days they will be happy—some days not. So while they practice the principles they know about, they leave to luck whether the principles they are not aware of will be implemented.

Certainly, implementing all advanced mirroring techniques, deep personality adaptations, and state optimizations is a rarity among salespeople. Great salespeople have the ability to implement many key sales principles at once, because the principles are deeply ingrained into their identities. This book aims to help you *become* a great sales consultant that constantly increases your sales capabilities.

Be Aware of All the Principles, and Increase Their Power.

To perform optimally, we need to optimize every principle as much as possible. There is a huge difference between simply believing in your product and being truly enthusiastic and knowing everything about your product. Each principle can be implemented to various degrees.

While the first step is to become aware of as many principles as possible, the second step is to raise the power of each principle. If you practice each principle as effectively as possible, you will be as great as you could ever dream.

This book is intended for both skilled sales consultants and new sales consultants. These sales principles will work for all types of sales environments, although they must be tailored to your unique sales situation.

As I began listening to sales training, I found that some sales trainers have better energies than others. Today, when information overflows in every part of our lives, selecting the highest-quality information is more important than ever. If we want to be the very best, undeniably, we have to learn from the very best.

The principles in this book are based upon the principles that I learned from other top performers, in addition to new perspectives I found myself that helped me to perform optimally on a consistent basis.

Three Simple Rules for Sales Greatness.

If you understand these three simple rules and apply them completely, you will have complete freedom in the world of sales—to do whatever you want and to manifest the successful sales reality you desire.

The first thing I learned in my first sales job was that everything can be learned—especially in sales.

Three simple rules.

1. Find and understand how to apply all the success factors in sales. Listen to sales training for two hours every day, and learn from the greatest people.

2. Understand why these success factors make customers want to buy your product.
   When you understand why they work, you'll practice and remember these principles a lot better. Understanding the principles lets you see the essences of selling forces, and once you understand these essences, you can create your own principles and focus on the ones that work well with your personality, industry, and sales environment. You'll also find and implement other principles faster.
3. Optimize the success factors as much as possible.
   Learn about the principles. Continue listening to sales training, and if you hear the principles in different or reformulated ways, that will only help the ideas sink in deeper. Don't take the principles you hear at face value. Think about them for yourself. Ask how you can use each principle in an even more powerful way. Practice them, and feel free to be creative in your sales optimization.

How Can You Make Your Sales Success Inevitable?

1. Listen to quality sales training for two hours every day, and completely integrate the principles you hear.
2. Give each sales conversation your full effort, just as a top athlete always gives his or her full effort on every play.
3. Philosophize for thirty minutes every day. What did I do right? What worked? How can I become even better? How can I become a truly optimal sales consultant? How can I reach this *specific* goal?
4. Every day, and as often as possible, visualize yourself as having already achieved your dream goal. Enjoy it.
5. Have as much fun as possible, and enter a state of flow as often as possible.
6. Make customers feel good in various ways. (Respect them and see the good in them, find commonalities, mirror them, have fun, and send positive energy.)

7. Believe in your true sales abilities.
8. Choose to sell a product you are interested in; the more interesting you find it, the better.
9. Listen to the best salespeople in the world. To reach the top, you have to be pointed toward the top, from the top.
10. Write down what's working, and treat what you write down as a foundation to build upon.
11. Watch inspirational videos every day.
12. Create a morning routine. Your morning routine can consist of going through incantations (telling yourself that you love yourself with feeling), visualizing your success, writing down your most important goals, and showing gratitude for what you've achieved thus far.

Remember:

You can always maximize a sales principle even more.

The Advantages of Being a Great Sales Consultant.

- You enjoy your days even more.
- You smile, engage in enjoyable conversations, and have a great time.
- You experience higher levels of achievement and can throw your hands in the air and celebrate each time you hit a new record.
- You love the feeling of growth and feel joy in your life.
- You help your customers by becoming better and better and feel blissful when you go home after a great day.
- You make your customers' day because you are a charismatic person and they are grateful to have spoken with you.
- You love seeing the sales principles you couldn't see before, and you are able to create in your head a more detailed map of where you want to lead the conversation.

- You look forward to learning even more and increasing the repertoire of skills in your arsenal.
- You have a deeper understanding of the fundamental principles of selling, and you understand that they are even more important than you previously thought.
- You become even better and surpass your own records, which makes you feel absolutely blissful.
- You help those around you more and create new opportunities, such as getting promotions, selling your own creations, or selling something more high end.

Personally, I quadrupled my income in five months following the principles in this book, and so did my best friends following the same principles. No matter where you're currently at, these principles will take you to the next level.

After my first week of selling, I had made 20 sales, which was not a good start in my job. But with the help of these principles and ideas, I soon managed to get 187 sales in a week, to private customers who answered yes over text messages to receive supplements.

Telephone sales of health supplements (omega 3 and so on) might not be the most profitable business, but it was something that I was interested in. And since I was interested in it, I was able to maximize my sales abilities.

CHAPTER 2

How to Think about Your Product to Sell Effectively.

* * *

You Have to Be Interested in What You Sell.

*Effective communication is 20 percent what you know,
and 80 percent how you feel about what you know.*

—Jim Rohn

Interest often leads to knowledge. When you're interested in something, you gladly learn more about it and become an expert. Your brain also remembers much more of what you learn when you're interested in it. As a natural expert, you should still aim to learn even more about your product so that you have even more powerful arguments to use.

It's a lot more fun to talk about something you're interested in than something you are not interested in. When you are interested in something, the customer subconsciously becomes more interested as well. You see the effect your own interest level has on the customer's. This phenomenon can be explained by mirror neurons. Mirror neurons allow us to feel what we perceive others to feel. To a certain degree, we feel what others feel, and you can use this biological impulse to your advantage when you sell.

Sell something you are interested in. This may well be the most important tip of the whole book, and it will accelerate your career and your progress toward your goals by at least ten years. How deeply you understand the principle of selling something you're interested in will determine your job satisfaction.

Picture yourself on a moving walkway that extends into the horizon in front of you. Selling something you're interested in and passionate about is like the treadmill moving in the same direction as you while you run with a tailwind. In addition, you are well rested, have eaten well, and have lots of vitality. Your top speed will be much higher than that of someone running on a treadmill going against him or her with a strong headwind.

With interest, you will enjoy the journey, as you can talk about something interesting while you are selling, advance much faster, and reach subgoal after subgoal. Your goal might be to make a specific amount of money in a month, to pay down your mortgage, to make enough money to take a vacation with a loved one, to spend time with your family, or to feel confident in your own abilities. Skills are the building blocks of a great life. We need social skills and the ability to relate effectively with other people. Mastering the principles in this book will serve you well for life.

Incredible interest = Incredible power

Internal belief = Influence power

Your internal belief in your product will determine your power to influence the customer.

When you believe in your product, you sound more honest and genuine and less stilted. Your enthusiasm will show in a natural way. You will have more energy, and your customers will find you more enjoyable to talk to.

When you understand the benefits of your product, you automatically do most things right in a conversation.

Other principles are still important to implement, like mirroring, professionalism, empathy, understanding, and many others, but the core requirements of a sales conversation are covered when you are knowledgeable and enthusiastic about your product.

Still, as great sales coach Brian Tracy says, "You can't make your customer believe in your product any more than you do."

Even though we want to make a lot of money, and it's definitely OK to use a monetary goal as motivation, we can reach that monetary goal faster by focusing on helping the customer. People can hear whether you want to help them and whether you stand for what you're selling.

Modern, Elite Sales Consultants Focus on Helping.

The good news is that we can increase our own beliefs in our products.

1. Learn as much as possible about your product. Experience it in the best way possible, or listen to other people's experiences with the product. You need to be hyped about your product because when you're excited, you can just talk from your heart. While talking from your heart, you can also use effective sales techniques.
2. If after learning everything you can about your product, you aren't sold on its benefits and can't see the value in it, find something else to sell that you like more.
3. Be so great that you can sell whatever you want. Great salespeople are a rare resource. If opportunities don't present themselves, create them.

If you have a job selling something you don't like, it won't be easy to maximize your potential. If you can't sell something you like more, then continue to practice the other principles in this book until you find something else you want to give to others. You should sell something you can recommend to your mother or father if it's suited to his or her needs or interests. Giving something to your close friends or family that you know will make them happy is a great feeling. And if you can sell something like that to a customer, that also creates a great feeling.

If you are already selling something you believe in, you need to make the benefits and greatness of your product evident to yourself. To influence others in a powerful way, you have to be sold on your product as much as possible. Having this commitment to your product is called buying in. When you buy in to your product, others will subconsciously buy in to it too. Many salespeople don't spend enough time selling *themselves* on the product. In your lifetime, you have probably met someone who was 100 percent convinced his or her product was great, and you probably witnessed firsthand the power this belief has.

The best way to completely buy in to your product is to experience the benefits in a very real way. If you sell gym memberships, for example, you should go to that gym, train there, and enjoy the benefits of that training. You could also participate in group training sessions, bring friends, and have fun with it. By engaging so directly with your product, you *feel* the positive effects of your product, and your memories of these feelings will influence your conversation with the customer in a positive way. If you have built muscles and are in top shape, you will also embody the benefits of your product.

This extends to any other product you sell. If you sell Tesla cars, or any other brand, take the car out for an adventure, and create a few naturally compelling stories that have a lot of punch when talking to your customer.

Experience Your Product at Its Best!

Very few salespeople utilize opportunities to increase their positive feelings toward their products, which in itself is a principle to help them sell more. True, genuine, and positive stories are great to add when suitable in sales conversations.

If you sell something that helps people make money, then have an adventure with the money your product provides, or find creative ways to feel the benefits. You can also *imagine* or *visualize* the benefits. These feelings toward your product will come through and create a sense of contagious enthusiasm in the customer.

How can you increase your belief in your product?

How *much* can you increase your belief in your product?

A professional basketball player knows that he or she has to do more than just play basketball and that training doesn't stop when he or she leaves the court. Basketball players train for strength, quickness, agility, and skills off the court as well. They also strategize, make plans, and work to increase their mental capabilities.

No player can slam-dunk or make one hundred free throws in a row without training or practicing. To succeed in your sales conversations, you have to read and learn about sales outside of the sales conversations. You decide how good you are going to be.

Increase every skill that can be increased. No successful basketball player thinks, "Well, I guess that's just how it is: I was born exactly this athletic, and this good of a shooter." Basketball players treat their athleticism as a skill, as they do any other skill in basketball. In this respect, athleticism is the same as product belief. Belief in your product is just one skill.

The one who practices the most, and the most effectively, wins!

The secret to being the best in the world is to do something you love.

What dreams do you have?.

Perhaps you want to make twenty times the amount of money you make today, own your own house, travel whenever you want, invest more in yourself, hire a cleaning service, eat delicious, healthy food, realize yourself fully, have even better relationships, possess a sense of mastery of your craft, feel blissful, be completely in the moment, or enjoy yourself with all the pleasures in life. The requirement for having all this and more is simply to practice as often and as effectively as possible to make it happen.

The Most Effective Mind-Set in Selling.

The most effective mind-set to have is "My product makes the life of my customer better." With this mind-set in place, it is much easier to sell, because you're not thinking about selling; you're thinking only about making their lives better. That's why people buy and sell products anyway; people buy a product because they believe it will make their lives better. That's what all products are made for, improving the situation of the customer.

Focusing on this makes everything easier. Aim to make their lives better with your personality, kindness, and product benefits.

If your product is good, people will recommend it to others, making selling much easier for you in the long run (as compared to selling something that customers don't find particularly useful).

By helping the people around you, your focus will shift from you to them, and you will naturally become the best version of yourself. You will appear more confident, and people will sense that you're there to help them.

You will also receive positive energy back from people, not all, but many. But remember that receiving positive energy and enthusiasm, while nice, isn't the most important thing. Even if they don't reciprocate your energy, that's OK; you just like spreading it.

Also, when you do kind things for others, whether they know and appreciate it or not, you subconsciously allow yourself to have more success, because you feel that you deserve it. If you have done things that were not kind, simply forgive yourself and focus on giving value again. What matters is what you are doing now. At its core, success is the act of giving value to others, and the other measures we use for success—money, good feelings, respect—are all side effects of bringing value to people. Value = success = money.

Smart people proactively seek out opportunities to help others. In addition to having fun and helping others out, they create goodwill, which provides benefits later. The amount of goodwill among your customers or in your workplace can never be too high.

> *If you're not making someone else's life better, then you're wasting your time. Your life will become better by making other lives better.*
>
> —Will Smith

What Are the Benefits of Becoming the Best Sales Consultant You Can Be?

First of all, you have a better workday. You quickly learn that customers' responses are just that—responses. Nothing is personal. If the customer is kind, that's nice, but apart from that, you just do the best you can to optimize the way you help customers, and it's up to them whether they want to receive better lives.

The only thing that matters is your skill set. Everything is a skill, and everything can be learned and improved.

As you become better and better, you will look forward to going to work. Customers will give you praise for helping them with your product and say thank you to you. You will feel highly skilled, influential, creative, kind, and intelligent. You will love yourself and love life. Your lifestyle will change, and you will be free to do what you want. Most of all, your love for selling / helping people will only grow stronger.

Many of the sales will become obvious. Of course they are going to want your product; it is, after all, the best product, with the most benefits they can get, and they are lucky to get it. You enjoy giving it to them in a professional and fun way. At the highest point in selling, you'll find yourself in a wonderful state called flow. You'll become happier and happier, and you'll find genius statements coming out of your mouth at perfect times.

Flow is when you feel as if you are floating or surfing on your words and the way you say them. You are completely in the moment, and a mixture of mastery, evolution, purpose, and happiness rushes through you. When you reach the highest level in sales, you will enter flow for a long period of the day, every day, and absolutely love it.

When you actively learn how to become better—and then you become better—you are filled with satisfaction, excitement, and a sense of empowerment that can be described only as amazing.

If you work on your skills, reflect on how you can become even better, and decide to become the best you can be, then you can do anything.

Are You Going to Become as Great as You Can Be?

> *Why can't I be the MVP of the league? Why can't I be the best player in the league? I don't see why.*
>
> —Derrick Rose

Basketball star Derrick Rose said this before the start of his MVP season. That season, he became the youngest MVP in NBA history. This is a powerful example of a real decision—a decision to become the best. He believed 100 percent in his own ability. Somebody has to be the best, and the one who listens to the best sales training, practices what he or she learns, and gives all, will be that somebody.

How great are you going to be?

The best?

Even better than just the best?

Is there a certain goal you want to reach?

The limit to your potential is set by you. It is determined only by what you genuinely believe you can achieve. As long as you dedicate yourself to lifelong learning, your limit will always move upward. Do we really need to have limits? The truth is that we truly are capable of achieving optimal greatness far beyond what anyone has achieved before.

The easiest way to move your aim and self-belief higher is to visualize. When you visualize, you imagine all your dreams in complete detail, and live in the moment you want to live in, in real life. You can also visualize yourself working effectively, listening to sales training, and enjoying it whenever possible.

In addition to visualization, you should practice and become better, and give your all when working. Practice in and of itself increases self-belief and makes you take even more action. With greater self-belief, you can and will set your goals even higher.

This process will eventually create a positive success spiral. You will become even more enthusiastic, reach new goals, listen to more sales training, practice even more, and then visualize and set even higher goals. When you have reached a goal, you naturally think, what is the next goal? What can I maximize even more?

Success begets success.

Dream Your Natural Dreams.

Allow yourself to fantasize and dream. As children, we do this naturally. Those who achieve big things have visualized big things.

Remember you are a special person with special talents, and you can learn anything.

Begin with this:.

Imagine that you are an optimal sales consultant, and get totally immersed in your vision. What do you see? See the details around you. What are you doing? Hear the sounds around you. Feel all the emotions that go along with that vision.

Be positive and full of gratitude, as if you've already achieved your goal. Live the dream and make it as optimal as you wish.

Picture yourself reaching your goal. Maybe you see a certain number on your daily sales overview or monthly paycheck. Maybe you see yourself hitting a sales number you once thought was impossible and throwing your hands in the air. Celebrate with total ecstasy and bliss, and enjoy having achieved your goal.

This visualization motivates your subconscious, linking pleasure to the achievement of your goal, and helps it to understand where you want to go. This visualization creates a path to success in your brain. When you have a goal, your brain sees that it will get pleasure from following through on the tasks needed to achieve that goal.

Another factor that makes visualization effective is that visualization actually shapes your identity. The reason for this is that your subconscious mind can't distinguish completely between imagination and reality. The more you visualize, the more your brain becomes familiar with the visions, and they become "you." We'll talk more about visualization later in this book.

CHAPTER 3

Realizing Your True Sales Potential.

* * *

Human Potential.

Remember that the potential of humans is incredibly high. Tiger Woods can hit a golf ball with enormous precision into a small hole hundreds of meters away. Men can squat four hundred kilograms. Musicians can create beautiful melodies. Think about all the different accomplishments of others that you admire. They are just people who have learned certain principles that work and have applied those principles until they succeeded.

Our potentials are truly immense. As a result, it's relatively easy to be a good sales consultant if you want to be. But if you desire to be the world's best sales consultant, the doors are open for that too.

PMA.

The most important thing in selling is the mental attitude you have toward everything.

PMA stands for positive mental attitude.

When you have a PMA, you are a person who smiles almost all day at work, and you look at what you do as a service to other people. You feel good about what you do; you enthusiastically enjoy it and have fun. You feel a sense of mastery in your occupation, you are committed to continuously evolving, and you see the meaning in what you do.

PMA is absolutely necessary in sales. You have to triumph over challenges, learn, and be willing to grow in any direction. While you work toward your dream goals, you can either have a positive mental attitude or not. If you do choose to have a positive mental attitude, you will immediately recognize increases in your creativity and energy levels, which influences the customer in a positive way and instills joy in yourself. With a PMA, you also have more energy, more confidence, and, by definition, greater focus on positive results. By focusing on the positive results you want to create, you increase the likelihood of them happening.

All the principles and processes of selling work *much* better with a PMA. So having a positive mental attitude is simply the right thing to have.

A PMA is something you are. You are a positive person, you see the best in every situation, and you constantly inspire yourself and those around you to do the same.

Even if you are already positive, you can up your positivity even further. People love other positive people because they give them back positive energy.

A PMA helps you stay focused on what's good and great and on constantly searching for new ways to become even better. A PMA also inspires faith in yourself and the belief that you can do anything.

WHEN SELLING, WE MUST APPLY A PMA TO THESE FOUR THINGS AND EVERYTHING ELSE: .

- The product
- Ourselves
- The transaction
- The job

The more we increase our PMA, the more effective we become.

So it is our job to increase our PMA as much as possible.

PMA regarding the Product.

The person who believes the most in the product is usually the best sales consultant in your business. Learn all the benefits of your product, and treat your passion for your product as a skill that can be amplified. Prove to yourself that the product is great and that your job is very important. Product belief is a skill that powerfully influences the customer. Your product belief is not simply strong or not strong; it can go from level 1 to level 100: the greater your belief, the stronger your influence.

You are not given a fixed product belief; you're free to increase it.

To increase punch in your conversations with your customers, experience the benefits of your product in the best ways possible.

Read about and watch videos about your product. By filling your head with positive information about your product, you will increase your positive feelings toward it as well.

Understand all the positive ripple effects your product gives the customer.

PMA regarding Yourself.

How much do you believe in yourself?.

Are you the most skilled sales consultant in the world? Are customers lucky to be talking to you? Are you a kind and charismatic person? Do you influence others in a positive way?

How much do you like yourself?.

Like yourself as much as possible. Only you decide how much you like yourself, and you are the determinant of your own self-worth.

You are the one who decides that you are a truly great sales consultant. You give away your product to massive amounts of people. Your personality and good feelings affect others in a positive way as well. As a sales consultant, you truly are extraordinary.

Forever increase your self-esteem by talking positively to yourself. Say to yourself, "I like myself," "I did this really well," "I did a great job there," "I am grateful for this," "Ha-ha, that's funny," "My work is truly meaningful," "I'm glad I gave this customer this product," and "I can do anything."

I still remember Brian Tracy talking about the power of saying "I like myself" again and again. Tell yourself that you love yourself, you love your life, you love helping people with your product, and so forth ten times every morning. Repeat these statements with feeling and conviction, and you will be amazed at the positive contribution this exercise makes in addition to all the other productive things you do.

Positive self-talk is really important for success. Pump yourself up for greatness. Talk to yourself as you would talk to your best friend. Use this power to self-motivate.

As you continue to learn and practice, let your inspiration shine within.

What are the advantages of believing in yourself?.

The more you believe in yourself, the more the customer believes in you.

When you believe in yourself, you're a lot more enthusiastic, happy, influential, and creative. All truly successful people have a fundamental, tenacious belief in themselves.

You have every reason to believe in yourself. You give your all, you are great, you become better and better, and you have already learned many things in life.

PMA regarding the Transaction.

Do you believe this is a good transaction for the customer?

Is this a sale? Is this a delivery? Will it make someone happy? Will it help someone? Are you giving good advice?

How you see the transaction determines how the customer sees the transaction, and it influences how many people you're able to help. Choose to see the transaction in the way that works the best for you.

Choose to focus on the value that your customers receive. Make sure that they are given the type of value they desire most. In each transaction, you are a true professional conducting a consultation with your customer.

People love to talk with experts who are genuinely trying to help them.

Why is it an advantage to be aware of how you see yourself and the transaction?

Because how you see yourself influences how others see you.

In all likelihood, the customer has never spoken to you before, so you have the opportunity to frame of the conversation however you want; actually, you can do this even if you have already talked to him or her before. People are used to allowing their perceptions of others to be shaped by how others perceive themselves, so you can determine how you want the frame to be, and it will be like that. If you believe in yourself and the product enough and back up this belief with results, you can decide how others view you and your product.

THESE ARE SOME OPTIMAL FRAMES TO ADOPT:.

- You are a true expert on this subject.
- You are passionate about this subject.
- You genuinely want to help the customer.
- You and the customer are friends.
- You like yourself, the customer, and life.
- The customer will be happy with your product.
- You are having a fun conversation.
- You are highly professional.
- You are happy.

Decide what frames will be beneficial for you to have, and create your own.

When you enter a conversation with the great frame you have chosen, and you act in accordance with it, the customer will often buy. But if you're not aware of the frame of the conversation, your performance will not be nearly as consistent or as great. When you understand your ability to effectively frame a conversation, you can be great on a consistent basis.

If you choose a friendship frame, you'll still have to introduce yourself, but the undertone of the conversation can still resemble friendship and familiarity, which can have a tremendous influence on the customer. Remember most of us probably have the same great-great-great-grandparents; we really are one family anyway, so it makes sense to act in that way.

An important note is that you should set the frame before you enter the conversation, so you adopt the frame immediately. Also, you can have several frames at once, like being a professional friend who is giving the customer this great product, and you will both have a fun time in this conversation.

How do you increase your belief in the transaction?.

First of all, consider and decide what kind of transaction this is. Go through all the reasons why this represents a good situation for the customer. As mentioned, you can also adopt several positive views of the transaction: you are a gift giver, an advisor, an expert, a buying accommodator, and so on. Find the most effective way of viewing what you're doing. And remember that since you have the power to define and frame each sales conversation, the way you see it is how it is.

PMA regarding Your Job.

Is your job fun?.

Always focus on the positive things. Try to find everything that is positive about your job.

What makes your job meaningful?

In what ways do your customers receive value?

What do you like or find interesting about your conversations?

What do you enjoy doing in the conversation?.

- Mirroring the customer?
- Discovering needs?
- The psychological aspect?
- The creative aspect?

- Being in a state of flow?
- Having a good time with the customer?
- Being enthusiastic and inspiring the customer?
- Feeling good about the positive contributions you can make in the life of the customer?

Do you love the feeling of growth and mastering selling?

Do you find it fascinating to learn?

Do you like that you can be social?

Do you enjoy influencing your results?

Do you like being creative?

Do you enjoy that each sale is both an art and a science?

Do you love riding the flow and finding yourself in that state more and more?

What makes your job fun?

Why is it important that you do this job?

IN CLOSING:.

By increasing and crafting your PMA in massive ways, you create a force that pushes and accelerates you forward, and it's your responsibility to shape this force and make it as effective as possible.

You have the strongest PMA regarding your product. You are a great sales consultant. It's your job to have a PMA toward your customers, a PMA toward your colleagues, a PMA toward your leaders, a PMA toward selling, a PMA toward yourself, and a PMA toward campaigns. All PMAs increase results.

When you embrace a PMA, you give yourself the power to optimize and change everything you can do something about. The things you can't change you can still have a PMA toward, because even though you may not be able to change something right now, you may be able to change it one day, or change how you view the situation. A PMA is just a tool.

Think about All the Benefits of Your Product That the Customer Will Enjoy.

It's vitally important to focus on the value you are bringing the customer. Always think about, feel, and understand the benefits the customer will gain from your product. If you are talking to a customer, and your only intent is to give him or her the best possible value, then this goal permeates the whole conversation in a positive way. The intention behind each communication should always be good hearted. While you can have other motivating forces, such as fun, mastery, learning, evolution, and passion, these should be used only to fuel your main purpose: to help the customer. Your good, helpful intentions are what should shine through your communication and create the undertone of your whole conversation. The customer loves this.

Customers feel and understand where you are coming from. They can feel when you genuinely want the best for them, and they will trust you more when you do. Empathy will automatically shine through when your tone embodies a "customer value first" mind-set. This mind-set will allow you to focus 100 percent on customers and see their needs more clearly, allowing you to tailor your presentation better to their needs.

With this focus, you will talk as if you know your stuff. You will talk as if you care about the subject and the customer. Your presentation will come alive and appear spontaneous and real. You will become more creative, and you will spend your time on the right things, becoming happier and more engaged. This mind-set increases self-esteem. You become genuinely interested in the customer and what he or she is saying. This, in turn, increases your flow state.

So focus on helping the customer and the benefits he or she will get by using your product. Let this be the dominant thought in your conversations and presentations.

This way of thinking is the most efficient and creates long-term, personal meaning in your job.

Ask yourself, how will my product improve the life quality of my customers, and how will it make them happy? No matter what you sell, you should ask yourself that question. With this mind-set, you automatically say many things right in terms of correct sales techniques.

CHAPTER 4

Fundamental Energies in Modern Sales.

* * *

Life-Force.

LIFE-FORCE IS A POWERFUL FORCE in selling. People often buy not only the product but the state you are in. If you have vitality, talk in a self-controlled manner, radiate positivity, and feel good while being enthusiastic about the product, you will have a powerful influence on the customer. Subconsciously, the customer connects your state of being to how he or she will feel when using your product.

The sales consultant represents his or her product, and in the eyes of the customer, the sales consultant is part of the product.

Remember you must learn to tailor your mood to the situation. In some situations, it makes more sense to be openly energetic, while at other times it's best to be calm. You should also be yourself and accept that you will be more or less energetic depending on how you feel. Energy is always good, but it can be self-monitored and self-controlled. Your energy can be either in the background or at the forefront of the conversation.

Enthusiasm is something you should have all the time, but not all enthusiasm is equal, and different kinds of enthusiasm are useful in different scenarios. You can be enthusiastic like Tony Robbins or enthusiastic like Steve Jobs. Both men have passion and energy but express them in different ways on stage. The more passion and energy they have, the better, no matter how much enthusiasm is shown.

The better you feel, the more products you sell.

You can increase life-force through healthy eating, sleeping well, being on purpose, training, and having fun. The better health you have as a sales consultant, the more energy and influence you have.

Improve your life as a whole. The positive things you do away from your job will positively impact your self-esteem, which you take with you into the sales environment. You can sell no matter what, but make sure you proactively make your life as fantastic as possible.

- Laugh.
- Have fun.
- Drink enough healthy fluids.

- Eat healthy.
- Sleep enough.
- Remember what you're grateful for.
- Set goals you are passionate about. These goals should have widespread positive effects for you.
- Be positive and spread joy.

Life-force and happiness sell. People want them and admire them, and they will want to feel the great feelings you are feeling. When you embody the feeling your product will give the customer, this will increase the chances of the customer buying. Do everything you can to be happy, but remember that happiness starts with a decision to be happy. Happiness is simply "I allow myself to feel happy now."

A very important point here is also to be as kind as possible to the ones you love and others. Relationships are a paramount part of life, and those around you deserve it anyway.

Life-force positively influences every other skill in selling.

Decide to be filled with vitality!

SELF-ESTEEM.

Your self-esteem is dictated by how much you like yourself. The most important step in building self-esteem is to decide to have great self-esteem. Take a moment to think about all the good things you do for others and how great you are. There is so much good in you. You are inherently a great person. Feel the deep respect you have for yourself. You have experienced so much, and you have seen how much you have grown, learned, and done for others. Whenever you do something good for yourself or others, you feel better about yourself.

We like being around those who like themselves, like life, and feel good. When you like yourself, you say and do many things that automatically make other people like themselves more. People who like themselves focus on the positive things. They focus on the best in themselves, the best in life, and the best in others. So when you focus on the best in everything, you are actually helping others, because you see the best in them. You want to be friends with people who see the best in you.

Positive self-talk is always a good thing. Talk to yourself as you do to your best friend. Say that you like yourself—you do, so you should say it. Be happy about the contributions you make to others, and tell yourself about the great work you do.

The more you like yourself, the less you care about anything other than positive responses from your customers. You like yourself, that's all that matters, and you can use this feeling to achieve greatness in your life by giving value to others. This outlook leads to a lot more sales. If you can double your self-esteem, you will see a huge impact on your number of sales. But remember to be humble. Self-esteem is not arrogance. Self-esteem is the positive feeling of loving yourself because you are a genuinely great person, and you respect and like other people.

When you have high self-esteem, the words you say sound better. You overcome challenges faster, you work harder, and your determination increases. You smile more, laugh more, and truly enjoy what you're doing. Flow is also closely related to self-esteem.

If you are too self-critical, you'll never be able to enter a state of flow, where you become one with your work and the moment. It's fine to have high standards, but it's not the same as being self-critical. If you want to meet those standards, being your own inspiration and talking positively to yourself are necessary components you use to get there.

The Way You Open.

How you say "Hi" at the beginning of each conversation is very important. The frame of the conversation is set with the emotion and implication of your first "Hi" and the first few sentences you say. For this reason, we should always be ready *before* the conversation, focused purely on enjoying the moment and being enthusiastic about the product. The more confidence, enthusiasm, self-control, and warmth you have in your introduction and greeting, the better. You will learn to optimize this energy on command when you give your opening some thought and awareness.

The frame of the conversation is that you are handing over the product to customers, they are going to have a better day by talking to you, and their lives will improve because of your product. They are lucky to have been given the chance to talk to you. You are the leader in the conversation (think of yourself as a great, kind, and humble leader). You love yourself and life, and you're glad to be talking to customers and giving them what you have.

You are happy, purposeful, and enthusiastic. You are self-controlled and understanding.

You can be the first to say "Hi." Be proactive and speak clearly so they hear you from the start.

To avoid coming across as scripted or mechanical, you also have to be spontaneous with the intro. Don't be afraid to change it up, but if you find an intro that works, you can use that as a template with which to start, and add creativity to it.

When you are in the state of flow, your intro often becomes magically effective. Customers can hear that you are in flow. They understand that you are completely engaged and 100 percent focused, they naturally become excited to speak with you, and they like it.

New salespeople sometimes enter flow without recognizing it; suddenly, they notice they've gotten unusually good results that day, and they wonder why. When you understand how to enter flow, then you can be great every day. And like everything else we've discussed thus far, entering a state of flow is a skill that can be learned and optimized. The next time you find yourself in a state of flow, listen to your thoughts and record your feelings. Afterward, you can use these mental notes to enter flow quicker by saying the things you would say in flow.

The trick here is that it's quite easy to enter flow every day once you are aware of the feeling and what triggers it. Also, your standards should be that you enter flow for large parts of the day, every day.

It feels great talking to someone in flow. While flow definitely isn't a requirement for making a sale, it certainly is massively positive. Think of flow as a professional basketball player who is in the zone. Stephen Curry is in the zone almost all the time. When you are in flow, you can have many great conversations, one after another, and truly feel it.

Be conscious of creating a good "Hi." The secret to a great "Hi!" lies in the energy you project. You form the energy you project based on how you think and what you focus on. Your energy should be fueled by thoughts like "I love myself and life, and I am talking to you because I can help you in a great way. We will have a positive conversation and have fun."

You are also confident that you are going to lead the conversation and that the customer will improve his or her life quality. This person is going to buy your product and will feel lucky and will be thankful to have gotten it. This is going to be great. You look forward to every conversation because each one is an opportunity to give the customer value and reach your goals. When you are truly happy and confident and show empathy, you are the optimal sales consultant.

Be original. Don't follow the script and say the same intro sentence as everyone else.

FLOW.

WHAT IS FLOW?.

It's that feeling we've been talking about.

Synonyms for *flow* include *wei wu wei*, *in the zone*, and *state*.

I remember first reading about flow in a book about how to become a better basketball player. The author called it *wei wu wei*, and it was fascinating.

We operate in flow when our brains are fully on and in the moment. The brain functions faster (the world slows down), you say more genius things, you feel fantastic, and you know you can do anything. It's as if you have sent energy all around yourself and deepened the contact with those around you.

And like everything in this book, flow can be increased. You can increase the time you're in top flow, how long flow lasts, how easily you enter flow, and your base level of flow every day.

But first, it's important to remember that you don't need flow—you can sell effectively without it. Flow only takes you to the highest level.

HOW DO YOU TRIGGER FLOW?.

1. Visualize yourself selling incredibly well, and imagine and re-create how you feel when you are doing it optimally. Think about every time you've done a great job. Think about all the people that have enjoyed receiving the product from you. Focus on the things that make you look forward to selling and that make you sell as much of your product as possible.

2. Understand that what you do is benefiting customers. Meditate on all the benefits they will receive from your product and assistance.
3. When you have begun giving away your product—keep going. Continue.
4. Play a specific song each time you enter or find yourself in flow. Eventually you'll be able to use that song to trigger your subconscious mind to enter flow faster.
5. Have fun, amuse yourself, and see the fun in everything you are doing.
6. Continue, just give it your all, keep talking to people, and flow will come.
7. Use decisive words, and talk as you do when you are in flow. Action creates emotions.
8. Talk positively to yourself. "I am great, I love this, I love my life, this is fun, and I am a master of this." Pump yourself up.
9. Enjoy the moment, and be grateful for what you're doing. You're actually making a difference in people's lives, and you're great at it.
10. Just got a sale? Keep going. Let's go. Wait to take a break. Delay pauses. By continuing, you stack the momentum.
11. Prepare water, food, and everything else before work so that you can avoid distractions and instead focus on giving away as many of your products as possible. Having juices, smoothies, and bars ready is a great idea.
12. Give it your all the second you get to work. Start spreading positive energy both in the workroom and with your customers.
13. Move. Movement helps activate flow.
14. Be happy, enjoy what you're doing, and celebrate your achievements. If the situation merits it, raise your arms in the air and celebrate a sale or win.
15. Do something funny or unexpected, challenge yourself, and expand your comfort zone.

Of course, you won't have to use all these triggers; try as many as possible, use all those that work for you, and add more. Learning your triggers and understanding how to enter flow give you more control over your own flow and increase your sales potential exponentially.

BE BRAVE, AND GET OUT OF YOUR COMFORT ZONE.

Be brave, and don't be afraid to do what you have to or want to do. If you are working together with others in a call center, stand up or even dance a little, and get your coworkers to join you. Decide to be unstifled and have fun. You always sell better when you're unstifled and free. Your team members will also be thankful that you take initiative and want to create a positive environment.

If you need to give a presentation, give it your all and enter flow in ways that will be beneficial for you in that environment.

Remember that the only thing that matters is your results.

Be Natural!

Selling has been around for a long time. But modern selling isn't really even about selling. Instead it requires that you act as if you were gifting your product to your customers. Now we need to view what we're doing as giving our products to people and helping them. Your job isn't to sell; your job is to be enthusiastic about your product, to like yourself, to have a pleasant conversation with your customers, and to improve their lives. Sales techniques are added after this mind-set is fixed.

Talk with enthusiasm. Be genuine. Say what you mean. Above all, don't talk like a stereotypical old-school salesman. Talk directly from your heart in your conversations. Be yourself and be enthusiastic, and remember to use enthusiasm in a way that is appropriate for your situation, as well as a little more energy than you think is necessary.

Sales psychology will be the same for a long time, but the way you communicate and your internal mind-sets will adapt and change with time. This book covers principles that are in alignment with today's requirements for success. The tonality we use in modern times is the same tonality you use when talking enthusiastically to people naturally.

To sell, you just need to make customers completely understand the benefits of your product and show them that they will receive and value these benefits.

Be Immersed in Your Conversation.

Being immersed in your conversation with the customer makes your product more appealing, and your customer will naturally become more immersed in what you're saying. Live in the words you say when you say them. As you talk about something, see the pictures, hear the sounds, and smell the smells that accompany the words, and truly feel what you are talking about. Describe what it feels like, if that is natural and appropriate. Experience what you are saying, just as if it were happening then and there.

Immersion goes hand in hand with focus. Focus on your customer, focus on the conversation, and focus on what you're saying. Then you will find yourself automatically emphasizing the right things, and the customer will easily be able to imagine and relate to what you're saying.

The effect of what you're saying is much stronger when you are immersed.

HERE ARE FIVE WAYS TO EFFECTIVELY INCREASE IMMERSION IN YOUR SALES CONVERSATIONS:.

1. Consciously be immersed in what you're saying.
2. Learn even more about your product—the more you learn, the more interesting and engaging conversation topics you will have to talk about. It's like the difference between knowing one move in basketball and knowing thousands. You don't use them all at one time, but you can select better moves at appropriate times.
3. Learn even more about sales techniques and principles. If you have just learned something new, focus on it, and create a way to test it out. Adding new sales skills to your repertoire is fun, and it's even more fun to refine them. Having different techniques and maps in your head makes selling more fun.
4. In sales your intentions are often made manifest, so use your intentions wisely. When you believe something will work, it often will. When you think about what will increase the buying temperature of the customer, you often find an answer and can increase it more. When you find sales techniques that work, stick with them, and constantly add to them in new, novel ways.
5. Decide to say things in an immersive way. The benefit of saying something many times is that you become even more confident in what you're saying, so repetition has its benefits too.

Know That the Customer Is Lucky!

Remember that customers are lucky to receive your product. Your product is great, and it's the best in the industry. People receive enjoyable benefits from it. On top of receiving a fantastic product, customers also get to talk to you, an incredible person who is positive, is intent on giving them the most value possible, and will make their day.

Perfect Authority.

Always lead the conversation.

Generally, people like an authoritative figure. Consider a skilled physician. People want their physicians to be confident in the right course of action but also understand and show empathy for their situations. It's important to add warmth, along with strong leadership, to the conversation.

You are the action taker, and you are leading them toward an improved life. Be leading but not controlling. Be perfectly and kindly authoritative.

Be an authority on your subject, and involve your customers in the receiving process. Make them feel good, confident, and qualified to make the purchase.

Involvement of the Customer.

When customers say yes or "That's good" or agree with you, allow them to be involved in the conversation. When you let customers join the conversation and talk, then they feel that they have been a part of the decision to receive your product. In some sales jobs, you may need to talk a little more, while in other jobs, you may need to ask a lot of questions and focus on being a star-quality listener. Even if you talk a lot in your particular sales situations, you should make room for being a great listener as well.

When customers participate in the conversation, they feel that it was their idea to buy. Involvement increases buyer frequency and satisfaction.

Get Them to Agree and Say Yes.

When customers agree to something or say yes, the buying temperature increases.

If you are selling something that allows people to better connect with each other, you can say, "And human connection might be the most important thing we have. Most of our happiness comes from positive relationships where both people give to each other, so prioritizing this area is a smart decision." Who wouldn't agree with this statement? Then pause and let him or her answer yes. Make it natural.

If you sell, say, phones, romantic relationship coaching or teaching people how to form friendships and the customer agrees that human connection is important, then this is in harmony with your product, and the customer has also partially agreed to your product. You will have to explain the product more, of course, but getting the customer to agree to the general topic is always good.

If you are up-selling or cross-selling, you can say, "And it's really nice to have everything in one place. Then you get a discount on the total package price, you have one supplier to refer to, and we also provide you with the best content." The customer agrees to these statements and says yes, either verbally or in his or her head. You will need to say this sentence in a more natural way for your specific situation. Don't think about the sentence; think about the elements. Talk straight from the heart about the benefits, and it will sound real.

Creating partial agreement is useful if done in a natural and no-pressure way.

All you have to do is consciously get customers to say yes as many times as possible while focusing on what is best for them. Your intention of getting them to say yes, while nodding within yourself or physically, will influence your tonality, which in turn will influence them.

CHAPTER 5

Attitudes and Principles for Greatness in Modern Times.

* * *

Standard for Yourself.

Michael Jordan always measured himself against his own standards. Other players tried to compete with him, but Michael competed with his own higher standards.

Standards also tie in to identity, which we will cover later in the book.

Set for yourself standards that are higher than those set for everyone around you. It's always possible to utilize a market, customer group, or sales situation better than everybody else. Oftentimes your peers aren't even close to maximizing the potential possibilities present in their workplaces and selling situations. Set your own standard for what is possible. Usually you can make at least four times more than everyone else in a particular field. If you also look at the opportunities to sell higher-end products or become a leader in addition to selling, you could make ten to one hundred times what the others at that specific job are making.

In a workplace environment, things have likely been done a certain way for a long time, and this has created a certain norm. Both small and even huge adjustments in the way things are done can make a huge difference in the results produced. Innovation is always an option for those who allow this possibility. Since improvement is always possible, you find genius and novel ways of doing things. Maybe you find a new way to present, discover a new sentence to use, stumble upon on a new way to create attention, and so on. Optimize all sales techniques for your selling situation, and you'll see possibilities where others don't.

Innovation happens only when you are open to the idea that everything can be improved and made better. If you believe you can get many more sales than everyone else, this belief will inevitably lead you to have more-effective conversations and drastically increase your conversion rate.

Focus.

What are you focusing on?

Where do you funnel your mental power?

The best focus always pertains to a goal that inspires you in the moment when you are having fun.

IN GENERAL:.

Always focus on what is positive, and try to see the positive in everything that happens. When you focus on the positive, you create more positive events, and you train your brain to notice even more things that are positive. Once in this feedback loop, you will experience positive things, focus on positive things, and attract more positive results. Your brain is unfathomably smart, and it will create situations and make you take certain actions that will create the same feelings you are used to feeling. That's why it's so important to take control of this loop and focus on your goals and what you are grateful for. Decide to make yourself spiral upward.

In the moment:.

Always focus 100 percent on the conversation you are in. Give it all you've got, and focus on how happy the customer will be after you've made the sale.

Read and Acquire Knowledge from Successful Sales Consultants.

The most valuable use of your time is to increase sales per hour—to improve your skills and become more efficient.

Spend *a lot* of time and resources on learning in the beginning, and balance acquiring knowledge with selling in practice and thinking for yourself. Always check the knowledge you learn with your own sense of what is right, and decide whether to use it, but remain open to new information.

The biggest epiphany you should get is this: someone has actually done this before, incredibly well, and written a whole book/program about how to do it. You can get that knowledge and implement it and build upon it to develop and optimize your own results.

What others have done you can do better. Gain the knowledge. Pay any price necessary for knowledge. Knowledge is the recipe for doing what will make you money. So truly splurge when it comes to the best possible knowledge. If you have the right information, templates, and strategies, you will save years of work and be much more successful in what you do.

So combine the knowledge of other high achievers with what you find out on your own, because you are a genius in your own way, and you know how you can best succeed.

Would it be worth it?.

Only a small number of people invest in themselves, and they are the ones who are living their dreams. The moment you decide to invest in yourself, that's the moment you decide to have faith in yourself and your abilities. Some things you can learn on your own, but selling is definitely an area where it is necessary, and tremendously beneficial, to learn from others.

You can either pay a couple of thousand dollars and use the knowledge you buy to become a millionaire, or you can spend a lifetime attempting to acquire that same knowledge. People have already created programs, with entire lifetimes of accumulated sales knowledge, ready for you to ingest and put to work.

Some people don't see the benefit of investing a few hours before and after work to watch videos and listen to the best trainers in the world. But what they don't see clearly enough is that those hours go directly into your sales per hour. When you put in extra hours of training and research, you will make more money in the long term; you can travel and live the life of your dreams.

You can even invest the money you make and make even more, but it starts with acquiring the best possible knowledge.

Your return on investment is by far the highest when you invest in your own skills and your most valuable asset, your mind.

As a skilled sales consultant, you will earn at least four to five times the amount earned by other sales consultants who don't invest in themselves. One month's work as a skilled sales consultant is worth at least four to five months' work as one who doesn't invest in himself or herself. The difference only becomes bigger as time goes on, as you continue to invest in yourself.

Difference in skill is directly proportionate to how much people are willing to invest in themselves. You'll know how serious you are about your own personal development by how much you invest in yourself.

Since you are reading this, I know that you are one of the special ones who prioritize their professional growth, and you have already decided to have faith in yourself, your abilities, and your ability to learn.

Beyond simply becoming wealthy, there is another, even greater benefit you get from investing in yourself: you feel tremendous about yourself. Every day becomes a triumph. You like yourself more, your confidence increases, and you have more fun at your job. You create new opportunities for yourself. You earn and command more respect. You have better conversations. You learn that you can do anything as long as you keep learning. You can go on holiday whenever you want. You are financially independent. You love life even more. You can hire a cleaning service and a cook and outsource many of the unnecessary monotonous tasks that don't contribute to your success. You have much more time to do what you really want to do, your life keeps progressing, and you constantly learn more and more. Your dreams are a guide to what is normal for you. Your dreams represent what is right for you, because only you have your specific dreams. Let yourself love learning, decide to grow, and your success is guaranteed. Your life will become better and better.

Gather the very best sales books in the world from the best coaches in the world.

Ask the best sales consultants in the world what they do.

Listen to the best. Study them.

Think for Yourself.

Write down what's working and what you can do better.

Much of what I've learned in sales has been from one specific sales coach, other people who sold supplements, a few other sales coaches, and other team leaders. I followed mainly a few programs that I heard over and over. In my e-mails I will include recommendations for these specific programs because it makes a huge difference whether you choose the right programs. In addition to that, I read a couple of other sales books, but I eventually decided to consciously avoid sales training that I didn't feel was optimal. I refined the knowledge I did gain, and I integrated it into the many things I found out on my own. I also spent a lot of time writing down and recording the things that made people want to buy, which required me to evaluate myself well.

Ask yourself how you can perform better, what went great, and what can be done even better. Write down the ideas you get. Read what you have written down previously, and continue to do what works.

Hard Work.

Constant top performance is what is required for great results. Learn everything you need to learn, make this knowledge a part of you, and give your all every day.

I especially like the analogy Brian Tracy once gave: you have to put forth a lot of effort to make an airplane achieve lift-off, but after that, you fly.

It's much easier to fly, and you fly so much faster than when you're on the runway.

To be the best, you have to give a 100 percent effort every day, and you have to be prepared and energized every hour, all the time. Once you have routines in place, try to arrive a little earlier for your job so you have time to pump yourself up, do a morning routine, and keep your momentum going. You will be miles ahead of the others. The truth is that 99.9 percent of sales consultants don't work hard. If you have the same attitude toward your sales job as toward a job that pays an hourly salary, you won't get far. If you have the same attitude that a top athlete or musician has toward his or her craft, you will create your own destiny. And eventually, you'll actually have a much easier life that way—much easier.

Working hard is like being Michael Jordan, in his prime, playing against a third-division player from Sweden who tries to defend him. Michael Jordan might work harder and smarter, but he has far more energy, self-esteem, and fun in return. Meanwhile, the third-division player will not have a good time playing against Michael Jordan. And of course, Michael Jordan also makes a lot more money than the third-division player. With that money, he can live a much better life.

When you see all those differences, you see that hard work really is *much* easier than not working as intelligently, efficiently, enthusiastically, and "hard." When you reap the benefits of your progress, you can enjoy the benefits while continuing to grow.

You actually don't work so much harder when you set higher goals. You're not telling your brain to work harder, only to be more creative and figure out smarter ways to sell.

When you set high goals, your brain adjusts your happiness level upward because it knows that you have to be happy in order to reach that goal.

One principle that will show up when you aim for higher goals is the principle of taking your sales as self-evident. We will go through this principle later in the book, and it opens up the opportunity for you to reach a higher level.

Even if your goals are incredibly high, have faith that your mind will figure out a way to achieve them. When you become that person who achieves those goals, you will really feel great.

Putting forth enthusiasm and energy (hard work) is like paddling fast enough to catch the wave so you can surf it, rather than not paddling fast enough even to reach it. The smart thing is to catch the wave early so you can enjoy surfing it the rest of the way. You are still working when you are surfing, but you enjoy it so much more, and you make progress so much faster.

When you work hard (enthusiastically and smart), you enjoy yourself. And since energy and enthusiasm beget more energy and enthusiasm, your hard work will only inspire you to want to work harder in the future. Hard work is actually easy.

Choose to wake up a little earlier to prepare, and to go to bed a little earlier to compensate. Eat nutritious food, train, and create energy within yourself. Work when others take a break, and work a little bit longer.

I really don't think working overtime is a good idea. It can be fun if done occasionally, perhaps to enable you to hit a new record, but it's much better that you instead use those hours to improve sales per hour. Spend the time learning about your product, learning about selling, or improving your life.

You will become better simply by the act of selling and by finding new ways to do things in the moment, but the other elements of sales progress are just as important.

EFFECTIVENESS.

Effectiveness, like every other principle discussed in this book, is a skill you can leverage to improve sales results.

Talk to real prospects, give them all you've got and that little extra, but be effective.

Always have a 100 percent PMA and close several times if necessary. But if you come across someone who can't buy, finish the conversation fast in a polite way. Always use your time as if it's the most valuable thing you have. Do things fast.

Be quick—but don't hurry. It's about prioritizing correctly.

Simply working hard, in and of itself, will increase your income by at least 30 percent.

Hard/smart work will take you very rapidly from average to elite status.

Not many people in this world are truly enthusiastic and focused on optimizing their craft—that's why not everyone is successful. To be a success, you have to bring energy to what you're doing. When you increase the productivity you put forth every day, the road opens up in front of you.

Sometimes hard work can be hard, but primarily, it's great fun. Hard work is mostly about enthusiasm, the will to listen to sales training, writing down what works, and thinking for yourself.

The more you work toward becoming better, the better your results will be. Enthusiastic work can become inner wholeness, immersion, inspiration, joy, and passion. Doing something you're great at and experiencing growth is one of the most magical things in life. It is the embodiment of passion and living.

It's always fascinating to learn interesting information about your product or sales in general while knowing that you will be able to use that information to grow even further. The feeling of epiphany is so delicious and addicting. It's almost as good as giving your all while you're in flow.

If you want to live a great life filled with growth and the realization of every desire imaginable, it's up to you to make that life a reality.

Plant seeds of achievement, indulge in the fruits of your efforts as you go along, and create a life of growth, friendship, love, and happiness.

Pushing.

Some customers need a push to improve their lives. You know the benefits of your product, so sometimes you need to give customers more information in a new way.

You are not pushing. You are just helping people with your product. Some customers don't know enough about your product, and that's why you're there, to help them understand how it will improve their lives, how they can use it, and so on. Your product is something everybody on your list should have, and you just need to help someone understand it a little more.

Most people you talk to will gladly accept your product straightaway, but those who are a little more reluctant may actually be those who need it the most. Recognize and understand that someone might not understand everything about your product straightaway.

If customers say they are not interested, then that has nothing to do with you or them. It simply means, "Tell me why I should be interested" and "You have not yet told me a benefit that is of interest to me." Brian Tracy taught me this, and in my experience, it's a great mind-set to have. Therefore, try other benefits and talk more about what your product will give the customer. It might also be necessary to mirror the customer more.

However, sometimes you will do everything right, and customers will still not want to receive your product. In that case, find the real reason. There might be some questions they have regarding the product that still need to be answered. Ask questions to find out what customers really care about. Sometimes they will give you a hidden reason.

Some might just need a little inspirational boost to actually improve their situations. In that case, remember to do it with warmth.

Some customers may just want you to comfort them and recognize their concerns. If you fulfill this need in a natural way, customers will gain the confidence necessary to buy. They only want you to respect, understand, and comfort them so that they feel safe and know that you want the best for them.

Remembering that you are a team will create a tonality to underscore that you actually are a team. Customers need confident sales consultants to lean on.

How to Handle Objections.

The best way to handle objections is to make sure that they don't appear in your sales conversation in the first place. You do this by preparing a great, orderly, natural pitch that naturally answers the questions that might pop up at logical times in the sales pitch.

Consider creating a list of the most common objections and finding appropriate answers to each of them. Then bring up those points in advance.

This process will make the pitch sound even more natural and logical to customers. You will usually know when a typical objection comes up, so you can be creative and address that concern before they have had a chance to voice it.

With that said, objections can also be very positive. As a sales consultant, you are almost a mind reader, but only almost, so it's always a good thing that your customers actually say what's on their minds or what they have questions about. If the objection is genuine, treat it just like information. It's natural that the customer has questions.

Objections can be real or false.

A real objection occurs when the customer is somehow unable to use your product. False objections are phrases like "I'm not interested," which means either that you haven't made them interested yet or that they won't voice their real objections, which may be lack of money, not understanding the product, or not seeing the benefits.

It is also natural that customers say yes, yes, yes, and thank you all the way throughout the conversation without any questions because you are so clear and build up your pitch so logically that all their questions are answered. Other times, you will have to answer their questions.

No matter what customers say, you should interpret it as a question.

An objection = a question. When they object, they are really expressing wonder or confusion over something. They are thinking about something and want you to answer what they are thinking about.

Here are three easy samples for handling any objections, depending on the needs of the customer:.

1. Say, "That's a good question."
2. Answer the question directly in a way that he or she understands, and make him or her agree by saying yes. You can also make a customer say yes nonverbally, through your tonality. Making the customer say yes helps the conversation move along nicely.
3. Move forward in your presentation.

Or

1. Say, "That's a good question."
2. Show that you understand the question he or she has.
3. Relate to a third person who had the same question. Tell a story about a person who was thinking the same thing and why he or she decided to buy.
4. Give an answer to the question. Remember to speak as if you were him or her.
5. Naturally make him or her agree.

Or

1. Say, "That's a good question/point."
2. Understand the customer.
3. Understand the customer again.

4. Relate to a third person and tell a short story about why that third person decided to buy.
5. Answer the question.
6. Naturally make him or her say yes and agree, through your tonality.

PRODUCT KNOWLEDGE.

You should understand *everything* about your product. Period.

Even though personality is more important than product knowledge, product knowledge is still very important.

Set aside the time to become an expert. It's better to be an expert than not to be one, and expanding your product knowledge doesn't take that much time.

Everything becomes better and easier with product knowledge.

Read about your product for thirty minutes every day (or as much as possible). Videos about your product are also a great source of information. The best people to learn from are those who are genuinely fascinated with, or at least interested in, the product, as this interest and enthusiasm will rub off on you.

An important note on product knowledge: Always speak to your customers at a level they can understand, and try to relate the information to something they already know about. Use metaphors to help people understand and make your conversations more compelling and interesting.

If the person knows more about the subject, feel free to be more technical.

If the person is focused on details, indulge in more details and use more advanced terminology.

If the person wants to be very straightforward and to the point, get to that point, and focus only on the most important things and how he or she will benefit.

If the person appears very focused on family and relationships, share how the product has benefited those close to you and how the product will benefit his or her family in a positive way. You can say, for example, "I gave this to my mom, and I've since noticed that she is a lot happier, and that positively influences the family, if you know what I mean."

Don't lecture the customer too much about the product's details or specifications. The customer needs to be able to understand what you are saying, and will want to understand only if truly interested. For this reason, engaging the customer with fascinating information always leads to positive results.

When adapting to a customer's needs during a conversation, you should be willing to go off script and, temporarily, off topic if necessary, and then leading again.

Know your product. Read or watch thirty minutes of fascinating information about your product every day.

CHAPTER 6

Mind-Sets That Help You Create Your Own Closing Techniques.

* * *

Closing.

If you want to improve your closing ability, improving your sales presentation as a whole is the best thing to do. When you focus on optimizing the whole sales presentation and tailoring it to suit the specific needs and wants of customers, they usually buy, no matter which closing technique you use. If you do the work before the closing sentence correctly, the closing sentence will come out naturally.

The most important thing in regard to closing is where you are coming from. These words show the energies you should have in the closing phase, as well as the energy you should maintain for the rest of the sales conversation.

- Advising
- Inspiring
- Showcasing benefits
- Helping
- Guiding
- Leading
- Giving
- Optimizing the purchase

When you have these energies, you automatically say things in an optimal way. For example, if you think about how you can optimize the delivery for the customer, you automatically ask questions such as these:

"Do you like this color better or that color?"

"Would you like to have it delivered to your home address?"

"What is your address?"

All these questions, when spoken as a result of thinking about how to help the customer, sound natural and good. They lead to a close because you genuinely want to guide customers to buy the product in a way that produces the best results for them.

On the other hand, if you have just read some closing techniques and say them, it won't sound as natural. You know the difference. Power comes from being natural and focusing on which energies you are using and where you are coming from when you ask those questions. When you are genuinely trying to help in a logical way, you will naturally articulate great sentences.

I want you to think through how certain energies and states of mind create the right questions and how these questions sound.

Remember customers can hear it when you care for them and want to create the most beneficial situation for them. This builds a lot of trust.

A lot of salespeople do this backward. They first try to determine what to say instead of determining where those sentences come from.

When people hear a generic sentence that is spoken because it was learned, as opposed to being voiced naturally, it may trigger red flags within them. Some examples of sentences that are generic are "Would you like it to be delivered at ten a.m. today or two p.m. tomorrow?" and "Would you like it in blue or green?" When you say the exact same sentence as other sales consultants, who may previously have not been successful with this customer, the customer associates these negative feelings with you. But if it makes perfect sense to ask whether your customer wants it in blue or green, and you ask because you are genuinely trying to help the customer that does not trigger red flags and is only positive.

This is a huge point regarding sales techniques and closing techniques. It has to be natural. The psychology behind the sales principles will stay the same for a very long time, but the sentences will be changed. The key is to start with the energies and intentions, then let natural words flow out of your mouth, all the while striving to be unique in the way you say things.

This also applies to the yes, yes, yes, yes technique, where you get the customer to say yes several times in row. Just don't be so obvious. You have to have the intention of making the customer say yes, and then do it in a natural way. General sales techniques will continue to change year after year. The reason customers don't like generic sales techniques is that some salespeople focus too much on technique and manipulation and not enough on the energies behind those sentences.

Modern sales is all about *being* a great sales consultant, not about *acting* like a great sales consultant. Don't study how to *act* like one; study how to *be* one. Sales is really about being that person who has found or created a great product and tells other people about it and helps them get it.

Making the customer say yes will always be better than getting him or her to say no. However, asking many unnatural leading questions does not work. When you know the difference between ingraining principles into yourself and mechanically following techniques, it's a lot easier to implement principles in what you do.

A common improvement that sales consultants can make to improve closing ability is to go heavier on the benefits. Really raise that buying temperature in an effective way, and make the customer see the importance of those benefits and how his or her life really will improve as a result of buying your product. You can also show all the consequences the customer might experience as a result of not buying your product. Do this in a caring and serious way. You need to lay out all the ramifications of the decision, both good and, if desired, not good.

WHAT DO THOSE BENEFITS LEAD TO? WHAT DO THE RAMIFICATIONS LEAD TO?.

When you see the full picture of these benefits and link them to satisfying customers' needs, wants, and personal dreams, your questions and comments will flow naturally. Find out what customers care about most, and let them know how this product fits into fulfilling that need. The higher you go on that benefit scale, the more power you see the benefits have.

WHY IS THIS BENEFIT IMPORTANT? AND WHY IS THAT IMPORTANT? AND SO ON.

When customers see clearly that they will definitely have more pleasure in life after buying your product, they are closed. The point is just to make this click inside the customer and, when you hear the click, simply go smoothly through the close. That's it. Just ask for the sale in a way that is somewhat comfortable. Just like jumping into a pool, you don't need to take forever to decide whether you are going to jump; you just make your customer jump. In this case, he or she is simply jumping into a high-tech Jacuzzi or floating tank.

If you don't need to ask the question "Do you want it?" *don't*. When he or she agrees verbally or nonverbally to your benefits, simply say, "Great, what is your address?" or "Great, then you can just write your name here, and we will get started right away."

When you close, you should be decisive and confident. You are there to give this product to your customer, not to conduct a survey.

Go straight into the close when the buying temperature is very high. Don't pause before asking for a sale. It doesn't make sense to pause. You are leading the conversation the entire time, and you need to use the same pace when you go through the close as well. Unless you want to highlight the tremendous importance of the product, closing is no big deal.

Important elements in closing:

FOCUS ON HELPING AND OPTIMIZING THE ORDER FOR THE CUSTOMER.

This automatically creates genius closing techniques. You simply go through the process of making sure the customer understands all the benefits of your product, the consequences of not having your product, how he or she will use it, and how he or she would like to have it delivered and when. You are helping him or her.

FLOW THROUGH THE CLOSE.

To make the sales transaction feel natural, you should keep the same flow and energy as in the rest of the conversation as you go through the close.

TAKE THE SALE AS SELF-EVIDENT.

Your tonality and mind-set should underscore how self-evident it is that he or she is going to enjoy your product. When you ask for the sale, you should remember all the benefits and really feel how beneficial this is for the customer.

RELAX.

As you relax throughout the close, transmit an underlying feeling of enthusiasm that will make the customer relax as well.

BE CONFIDENT.

When you are confident throughout the closing part of the conversation, the customer can lean on you to feel safe during the buying decision.

BE HAPPY TO GIVE YOUR PRODUCT TO THE CUSTOMER.

Be happy during the close, but remain professional. You are really making his or her life better, so it's natural to be happy.

Use humor where appropriate.

Humor is a great way to increase relaxation and open our bodies and our minds to receive.

Talk as if you know this is a yes customer.

Expect the customer to say yes.

You have sold to many others before, and when you have a tonality that expects the customer to say yes, you subconsciously communicate that many other people are buying your product and that it is completely natural to buy from you.

If many other people have bought the product, let the customer know. Social proof still has an impact on people. Be enthusiastic and determined to give this to the customer.

In my e-mails, I will send you a couple of more samples of useful closing sentences. But remember that the most important thing in regard to closing is not the words used; it's where you are coming from and the energies you implement. When you focus on these, you will be able to create your own closing techniques.

Here are a couple of closing techniques:

Trial close.

The trial close is where you let the product close itself. Here, you just say that you can let customers test the product for a given period, then decide whether keep it. If they like it, they can pay for it, and if they don't like it, they can return it.

SELF-EVIDENT CLOSE.

Just say something like "So what you get is this, and it includes this and this, and it will be delivered like this. Is this your right address?" The whole key to this close is to take it as self-evident that they are going to accept your offer, and you talk like that. Specifically, what you say depends largely upon what sales situation you are in, but the intention will guide you through the close. If you can find a way to use this closing technique, then it can be very effective.

SIGNATURE CLOSE.

After you have gone through all the benefits and consequences of not buying your product, and the customer has agreed thus far, simply give him or her the piece of paper he or she needs to sign and say, "Great, I think we've gone through every essential detail of this. All you have to do now is sign here, and we will get started immediately." Say it your own way, as with all the examples in this book.

SUMMARY CLOSE.

This technique can be done before the signature close. In the summary close, you go through all the things the customer wanted and ask whether this is correct. The summary close is also a great way to get the customer to say yes several times in a row.

For example, "OK, this sounds good. Let's go through the details and see that everything is the way you want it. You wanted this, with these accessories, with this guarantee, and so on. Is this correct? Great! Then I need you to sign this, and we will take these next steps."

RECOMMENDATION CLOSE.

When you have positioned yourself as an expert and your customers respect your wisdom and feel that you care about them, you can recommend what you believe is best for them.

MAKING THE CUSTOMER SAY, "YES, I'LL TAKE IT".

Go through the benefits, and have an intention in your voice that makes customers say, "Yes, I'll take it." This may sound very simplistic and rare, but actually, when you do this right, you can really get the hang of it and be very skilled at making the customer say, "Yes, I'll take it!"

The tone you use, the benefits, the timing, and everything you do in your sales presentation can trigger that response: "Yes, I'll take it." Don't rely only on this type of close, but be aware that you can make a lot of customers say yes using this technique. Be intent on triggering that "Yes, I'll take it" response within customers. Once you have done this a couple of times, you will get the hang of it.

If you can get them to say this, it's just a bonus. If they don't, just close by yourself.

Also, keep in mind that when you are doing a great job talking about the benefits of your product, you should generate buying interest, and this will cause customers to ask for the price or delivery plans or other information about the product. Once they ask for details regarding the product, take this as a major indicator of high buying temperature, and go in for the close after answering the question.

SILENT CLOSE.

If the customer is on the verge of saying yes, be quiet until he or she says yes.

For example:

"How much does it cost?"

"This product, including the accessories and guarantees, will be…"

Silence.

Allow her or him to say, "Yes, I'll take it," or "Yes, thank you."

In my e-mails, I will provide more sentences you can use as examples of closing sentences. However, in this book the primary focus is to help you come up with your own closing sentences and focus more on where the words are coming from.

Sales closing techniques account for 1 percent, or a maximum 5 percent, of your ability to close sales. The best closing technique is to raise buying temperature.

Click here to get more tips, including closing phrases.

www.SellingGreatness.com

CHAPTER 7

Simple Keys to Optimize Your Confidence.

* * *

Confidence.

The more you believe in yourself and your product, the more confident you will sound. When confident, you say things in a self-evident way because you've already read about or learned the evidence behind your claims and sentences and you know they're true. You are not trying to sell anything but are instead just stating things as they are. You can increase your own confidence through learning more about the benefits of your product.

The more you believe in your product, the more the customer will believe in it. People enjoy buying from people who are confident in the value of what they are selling.

There are a lot of things you can do to increase your own confidence, like positive self-talk, incantations, goal setting, growth, doing high-value tasks like working on yourself, and practicing self-love.

You should do all those positive things, but in selling you should also have a lot of confidence simply from the fact that your product is great. These three powers of confidence add up to one energy of confidence:

1. How confident you are in yourself
2. How confident you are in your product
3. Knowing that you are improving the customer's life quality, so it's a great thing you are doing

if the customer says, "You're a good salesman," then you should respond with something like "Thank you, but it's really just because the subject is so important. I know that this product works, so I get very passionate when I talk about it." Then proceed with the pitch from where you were.

You are responsible for increasing your belief in the product as much possible. Belief will propel you forward and make you say the right things!

When you believe strongly in your product, you are really just calling to give it to them, and you seem very confident. People enjoy speaking with confident people and will follow your lead if they sense you have their best interests in mind.

Feel free to use phrases like "You're welcome" and "I'm glad I could help you." The customer will usually respond with "Thank you" and will have an easier time understanding that he or she is receiving something of value.

TRICKS TO INCREASE YOUR CONFIDENCE:.

1. You and the customer have never met before, and you can start the relationship any way you want. Set the frame right from the start. You can choose to be a consistently confident, funny, happy, leading, empathic, professional, and charismatic person who is calling simply to help and improve the customer's life.
2. Use confident language and say things in a determined manner. Use strong words and say that everything *will* truly work/help and so on.

3. Think about whom you would like to buy something from, and be that person. If you buy something and need help, then you want to be able to reach out to a capable person who can tell you *exactly* what the best choice is and why. You want to get along with the person, and you should be confident that he or she cares about you and the subject with 100 percent certainty.

Relationship.

In a world where we are more connected than ever through the Internet, a lot of people don't feel very connected in reality. This dynamic has made connection a bigger part of selling than in earlier times. We like to have a connection with the sales consultant. The faster the sales consultant can create a connection with the prospect, the faster a sale can take place. Laughing together, agreeing, and seeing similarities in each other are great ways to create a bond between the two of you. Also, it makes your job more fun when you genuinely connect with people on a regular basis.

A relationship, even for just five minutes, satisfies a need for human connection more in these times than previously. Connections have more value today, so this is an important area to focus on. When people can buy a lot of things over the Internet, they actually like the fact that they can talk to someone about their buying decisions, since there is so much to choose from.

When it comes to larger sales, spend a little more time to get to know the customer. When you ask questions back and forth and get to know each other more, this builds familiarity and trust. If you sell smaller products, you can still sell fast, but then you have to create connections more rapidly.

The most important thing to know about building relationships is the importance of actually doing it. If your friend recommends something to you, think about how much trust he or she already has with you. You are inclined to buy the product simply because the person has given you the value of friendship previously.

I am not saying you have to spend a lot of time forming friendships before presenting anything; you can focus purely on selling if you want to, but it's beneficial to add the friendship value as well. The point is that you see how beneficial it is and that you create it with a lot of different principles. In some larger sales, you might need to focus more on the relationship process before closing; it totally depends on what you are selling.

Another benefit of focusing on creating a relationship is that you focus more on your customer and appear more confident as a result. This focus invariably makes your job more fun as well.

Master the art of becoming friends with someone fast.

The most important principles for creating a positive connection are these:.

- Mirroring
- Warmth and friendliness
- Confidence
- Enthusiasm
- Positive energy
- Focusing on helping the customer
- Asking questions
- Being interested in the customer
- Showing empathy
- Having fun with the customer in a professional way
- Laughing together
- Making the customer feel good about himself or herself

Also, talking about things that interest customers is genius, but it must be done naturally. If you can say things you know they agree with, this creates a bond. If you can make them laugh, this is a powerful connection builder.

Find commonalities, but don't do the typical "Ah! Me too!" Let the commonalities come out naturally.

Professionalism.

Be professional. Embody a professional attitude, and help customers feel safe by projecting a confident aura and creating a professional environment. Subconsciously, they will associate this professionalism with your product. Have a relaxed attitude, filled with humor, enthusiasm, and self-control, and your total energy will be incredibly pleasant for buyers.

The best way to implement professionalism in your sales calls is to feel professional. Get in touch with the feeling of being a true professional by pulling back your shoulders, relaxing, and letting yourself become enthusiastic and happy. You can generate these feelings within yourself through your intentions and your body language. It's your job to lead customers to a better life. You have an important job to do. Try these things right now, and you will immediately notice that you can embody this professional state. Be yourself at the same time

If you focus on being professional, your calls will be more efficient, and customers will be more responsive and will actually want you to lead them.

You want your doctor to be professional, and you want your bus driver to be professional. In the same way, customers want you to be professional as well.

Dealing with a professional makes customers feel reassured and as though they're in good hands.

The conversations where your professionalism shines through are usually the ones where you get the largest orders.

People like to buy, and they certainly buy as much as they want when they can lean on a true professional. If you sense that customers might want to buy a lot, you can inspire them to go all out. It's the best thing for them anyway, and they may even qualify for some discounts by making a larger purchase.

Many customers want to buy and love buying a lot—much to your benefit—but this is all based on both you and your company's ability to inspire confidence and trust. Only with your sense of control and confidence will they allow themselves to buy what they truly want and need.

Professionalism also increases the value of your product—that is, how much customers feel that the product is worth. Because you are a professional, they will subconsciously view your product as more professional.

Enthusiasm.

The best type of enthusiasm is a self-controlled type of enthusiasm. The difference between a pot that boils over and a pot that cooks perfectly with the lid on is huge. By keeping the lid on, you can increase customers' willingness to buy in a significant way while also ensuring that everything remains under control during the buying process.

This type of enthusiasm is also the most contagious, since it will inevitably seep into your selection of words, pressure, and intonation occasionally. Let a video of Steve Jobs talking serve as a good example of self-controlled enthusiasm.

This does not mean that you can't be free or open or let yourself loose. You should absolutely be free and willing to shout if you want to and if it suits the conversation.

If you make a sale, you can raise your arms in celebration, and people will love that. People love when others are authentic, and they feel good when others allow themselves to be open and energetic.

THE IDEAL TYPE OF SELF-CONTROLLED ENTHUSIASM IS WHEN THE CUSTOMER PERCEIVES THE SALESPERSON LIKE THIS:.

"He is not trying too hard or anything. He is simply professional and talks naturally, but I can tell that he is genuinely enthusiastic about what he is talking about!" When the enthusiasm bursts out here and there and you naturally punctuate certain words, you will have a powerful affect. Just let your enthusiasm flow naturally. If you have done a great job researching your product, this enthusiasm will come naturally to the surface in your conversations.

Embrace a naturally energetic and great mood by doing and thinking specific things that you know will boost your state. Show enthusiasm in what you do. Enthusiasm is the factor that accounts for the bulk of the sales you make. The old saying "A sale is a transfer of enthusiasm" is as true today as ever.

Let your enthusiasm flow by believing in your product and yourself, and pump yourself up with inspiration.

A lot of people aren't used to being around enthusiasm, so they love it when you come into their lives with enthusiasm and provide something for them to feel enthusiastic about. Everyone enjoys a bit of enthusiasm in his or her life, and this character trait is definitely one that everyone admires. Enthusiasm is contagious and, in addition to catching their interests, will make clients more enthusiastic about enjoying the benefits of your product.

A CLASSIC EXAMPLE IS THIS:.

If a friend tells you about a movie he thoroughly enjoyed, that will have an impact on you. You might become a little tempted to see the movie if your friend simply tells you about the plot. But if your friend says he thought it was one of the best movies he's ever seen and appears very enthusiastic about it, then this attitude will have a much stronger impact on you. It may be the deciding factor in whether you actually go see the movie.

If you are able to make a habit out of being enthusiastic all day, you'll be able to close *a lot* more sales. You'll love feeling passionate and alive. It will make a *big* difference. Some people are in an enthusiastic state of mind only for a few minutes—or hours—during the day yet still do quite well. But those who are able to stay enthusiastic throughout the day—that is, for eight hours—have earned a *huge* advantage.

WHAT YOU CAN DO TO INCREASE YOUR ENTHUSIASM:.

- Think about how good your product is.
- Think of all the benefits you will bring your customers—think about how lucky they are.

- Remind yourself how much you like yourself, and say it out loud. Think about all the good you have done for your family, your friends, and others.
- Think about how much you enjoy giving your product to people.
- Move. Jump up and down, clap your hands, dance—just move. This will increase your energy and positivity, which will in turn affect your level of enthusiasm.
- Get enough sleep. You can perform well no matter what, but enough sleep always helps.
- Eat healthfully and keep your energy up. Caffeine is an old trick that still works, but feel free to try some green tea instead of coffee. If you already drink tea, make sure to get enough iron to offset the tannic acid in green tea, which inhibits the absorption of iron. Green tea also contains L-theanine, which makes you feel more relaxed, so it's an all-around better way to get your caffeine kick. Plus, it's healthy. Three tea bags of green tea equals one cup of coffee.
- Drink enough water.
- Have fun. Enjoying yourself will generate better results. The power of enjoying yourself is tremendous and will give you control of your own destiny as you move forward in life. Find things that are fun, and try to see the fun in things around you. Don't take yourself too seriously either.

  LeBron James, one of the best basketball players in the world, once said that he was not able to achieve true success until he started enjoying himself while playing basketball. After he started focusing on having fun, he won several consecutive championship titles.
- Set goals for yourself that encourage you. Have an inspiring goal that you keep in mind, and set subgoals as well.
- Create small competitions for yourself and others. For example: Who can close a double sale first? Who can make the most sales within a given period? Set multiple subgoals for yourself to check off. Subgoals will increase enthusiasm, keep you motivated, and generate more

frequent feelings of achievement because they create several small triumphs leading up to your big achievements.
- Watch inspirational videos or listen to or read inspirational material. You can listen to interviews of people who inspire you that give their keys to success. Find out what inspires you, and subject yourself to this inspiration as often as possible. The best inspiration is rooted in yourself and your own unique dreams. Remember there's a reason why you, and no one else, have your specific dreams. They are yours.
- Be the best you can be. Improve, develop, and master your skills and who you are. Keep learning and take even smarter action.
- Set clear, key objectives. Set goals that will give you positive results in the most important areas of your life, and achieve them. You are better off achieving goals that lead you on the fastest path toward the realization of your dream than you are cleaning your house. Divide your goals up into smaller goals, and celebrate the achievements of each of these subgoals as they lead up to your ultimate goal.

Imagination is the preview of life's coming attractions.

—Albert Einstein

Amplify Emotions.

Emotions are the driving forces in sales. People's logic is not truly logical, because what they feel most strongly about is not necessarily the most logical, even though they may believe it is.

There can be a thousand different reasons for why something is important. As you talk to many different customers, you will see this clearly. There are no logical reasons; there are only multiple different reasons for why people do what they do, based on their feelings. Once customers have attached emotions to specific reasons for what they are doing, they'll automatically think that this constitutes logical reasoning.

Customers have lived lives full of different events that make them all prioritize different things. Some people think it's logical to choose the safest thing to do, some choose the most exciting thing, some choose the thing that will give them the most connection with other people, and some choose the thing that will help them grow the most or the thing that will most positively contribute to others. Many different reasons can be the most logical one. People also think combinations of different reasons are logical.

Build up the conversation so that it revolves around the feelings you believe the customer cares most about. Talk about how the customer will feel and what positive effects that will lead to. By tapping into these feelings, you create a lot of interest and capture their attention.

When you do this, talk about their feelings in the way they would have said it. When you can speak what's on their minds, you automatically earn tremendous credibility because they feel that you understand them.

You can use this tactic by thinking about what customers might be thinking and then saying it in the conversation. Try to be a mind reader of their pasts, and then mirror them, "be them," and say sentences you believe they have previously said to themselves or will say in the future.

Some people value safety, so amplify customers' emotions or mention other customers who have been satisfied with the safety regulations, the professional engineering, or the feeling of being safe they got. You could also mention an authority that supports the product, because authorities can represent safety. Authority-based arguments are a positive contribution to a sales pitch in almost all sales situations.

If customers are concerned about performance, talk about how well the product will work for their specific needs and help them perform and achieve their goals.

Talk about how your product is good not just for customers but also for the people surrounding them.

This works especially well with customers who talk a lot and have a tendency to ramble. These are very people-oriented and family-oriented people, and they feel more than they think. These are customers who value communication with people and use conversation as a tool to connect with others. If these customers see that they are able to gain connections and communicate better with those they love by using your product, then that will surely suit the needs and emotions they care about. Effective selling is all about understanding those people and getting a sense of what they feel is important.

Another good tip is to become a bit emotional yourself, in a positive way.

Apply your emotions to the sales conversation—this will bring life and importance to the conversation. People like it when others share their emotions. You can also let yourself be enthusiastic about the benefits of the product and how important they are. There is a reason why people watch movies; it's because of the feelings they can create. Feelings make the pitch fascinating.

NEEDS.

Always emphasize your product in a way that meets the needs of the customer.

Anthony Robbins has a nice blueprint for human needs that goes like this:

There are six needs:

- Certainty
- Uncertainty/variety
- Connection
- Love
- Growth
- Contribution

Take a moment to search for *Six Human Needs* by Anthony Robbins.

Understand these principles, and you will have even more leverage when you want to *move* people.

I feel that this simplified model is very useful and applies to many people. Naturally, people have many more needs than Tony mentions above and more specific ones as well. These are, however, pretty universal, and they can therefore serve as a basis to find needs effectively.

First of all, it's a good idea to find out what customers care about most. If you then present your product in a way that makes customers believe they can meet one or more of these needs with the help of your product, they will buy your product. If you can focus on selling them on their primary needs, that is great. Some people will have very obvious needs, and you will easily see which ones drive them.

REMIND THEM OF THEIR NEEDS.

You can find a customer's specific need by allowing him or her to tell you what it is, by using questions to identify it, or by gambling on a need that the customer might have.

Questions are great. Sometimes, during shorter calls, when you are doing high-volume work, reminding a customer of a need you think he or she might already have is a good way to do it.

You still have to ask some questions, and then you'll have to make an educated guess as to what need you should focus on. Oftentimes, you'll know that 90 percent of customers have a specific need, and you can just begin talking about that if you have to be effective and efficient in your sales pitch. When you have more time, however, you should always complete a thorough needs analysis and use laser focus to find the most important driving forces of the customer.

When using this method, you can also disarm many objections beforehand. You can talk about the objections you know will come up before the solution is presented, and solve them before they surface. Using this strategy, you can create the sales pitch in a very natural way. It's like tossing a baseball perfectly up in the air before hitting it.

Of course, there are ethical considerations you must make regarding creating a need within the customer.

Mirroring also fits very well inside this principle. When you say what they would have said themselves, then it's really powerful, and they recognize their needs more easily.

When you have first taken customers to the need in their minds, take them further to the solution, then to their dreams, then to all the ramifications, then to the reasons they should buy. There are more steps than that, but you get the point. Create a seamless pitch that answers the questions customers may have before they even come up.

If you find a need, remind them of how important it is to fulfill this need.

Naturally, you will tailor your presentation in a way that fulfills the customer's need, but you must also remind him or her of how important this need is.

Another important element of the job is to remove the fear people might have about saying there is something wrong with them. Some people have no problem complaining about their issues openly, while others are more hesitant to admit they have a problem.

The older generation also has a desire to remain young and in shape. By saying that the problem is "very common in this country" or that "I've used it myself," I let any given older customer feel as if he or she is just one of many and that the problem is common and OK. This will help customers open up to you more. If you just say, "You're probably not in too-good shape, right?" customers will, of course, not open up to you. Some needs and problems can be protected and hidden by their egos. For example, if you sell energy products, they will say, "If I get too much energy now, I'll jump through the roof," or something like that, because they want to save their egos.

To disarm the objection before it shows up, you can give their egos an excuse: "People have so many obligations now. They care for their families, work too hard, and work overtime. Some have children they need to look after. They try to train when they have timeh, but sometimes they just get tired. And they want something for more energy, which is why Dr. Bernt Ole actually created a natural energy supplement with…"

Of course, you have to say this line naturally and hit hard on the benefits afterward. In a complete sales pitch, this will sound better, with more context and natural speech. But the idea behind the words is that if customers now admit to being a little tired and in need of some energy, they are also admitting to being hard workers, taking care of people around them, and giving their all. In that context, being tired can actually be positive for their egos. So remember: before presenting a solution, remind them that they have this need.

In order to prepare your customers to mentally accept your information, you need to find out what your customers should hear before you start your presentation. If you repeatedly receive many objections at the same point in your pitch, plan to say something in advance that responds to the objections if they occur often during this specific point of the sales conversation. I've learned and built upon this principle from Brian Tracy.

Being Authentic.

Be yourself. Other people love people who are themselves. The reason is that this allows others to be themselves too. The modern salesperson is fully himself or herself, and the salesman persona is long gone. Customers should not think of you as a seller when you talk to them. You should present yourself as a kind person who simply says what he or she means and is there to help the customer.

Don't be "something"; be yourself. Say what you mean, be honest, and talk in a tone that is uniquely yours.

At the same time, use techniques to control the intensity and speed of what you say.

Always adjust to your client, but remain yourself. This will create a genuine emotional connection between you and your customers. When you become an advanced sales consultant or thinker, you see that certain principles overlap but are still both valid. By "overlap," I mean two principles can be contradictory but still both be valid at the same time. For instance, you can be fully yourself and mirror at the same time; this is an overlap. These are three examples of principles that overlap but are still all valid:

1. Being yourself
2. Using techniques
3. Mirroring the customer

Start by being yourself, and then realize that you can be both energetic and relaxed, so therefore you can adjust this parameter of yourself. You can also choose to be happy or not happy, so you can adjust this too (but let it come naturally). You can also decide what to say; therefore, how you set up your conversation is a technique. There are many techniques you can use, and you can adjust your own energies to make them more effective in selling while still remaining completely yourself.

You can both be yourself and mirror the customer at the same time, because "you" are neither your dialect nor your speed and tone of voice. These elements of your speech are totally random. You randomly grew up where you did and listened to those around you, and this made you form a dialect. Much of your personality is also random. Still, there is something that is "you." So you can freely adjust your style of communication to jibe better and more in sync with the other person while still being yourself. You can talk slower, faster, higher, or lower and choose to use mannerisms that the other person uses as well. Again, do this in a natural way. It can be very fun.

When you talk about your product, be straightforward and tell it like it is. This way, when you say that it is a truly great product, customers will know that you are telling them the truth. They, in turn, will be open and honest with you and tell you what their needs are. They will be more open to your pitch, and they will listen closely to what you say. They will simply be more likely to buy your product because you are yourself.

Authenticity, being yourself, has its own value aside from the product, and it's widely recognized as a great character trait. The large majority of people are not open enough and are somewhat guarded, but they tend to be positive and enthusiastic when you talk to them while being entirely yourself and simply saying what you mean. This is truly something that everyone admires. Just being with you and connecting with you will provide them with additional value.

When people are truly themselves, they build trust.

Mirroring.

We like those who are like us. Like attracts like, and complementary energies also attract each other.

While being authentic, you should mirror at the same time. If you are in a full state of flow and are fully expressing yourself, you may need to mirror only minimally. But even so, you will benefit from mirroring. In mirroring, the people you are talking to should feel as if they were speaking to someone nearly identical to themselves.

A connection should be made wherein your communication hits their wavelengths and you synchronize. You should talk as if you were on the same energy wavelength as customers. They should feel as if you and they were one and the same—as if you were your customers and they were talking to themselves. Say things that you think customers would say in the same way that they would say it. Think like them, and then naturally talk like them.

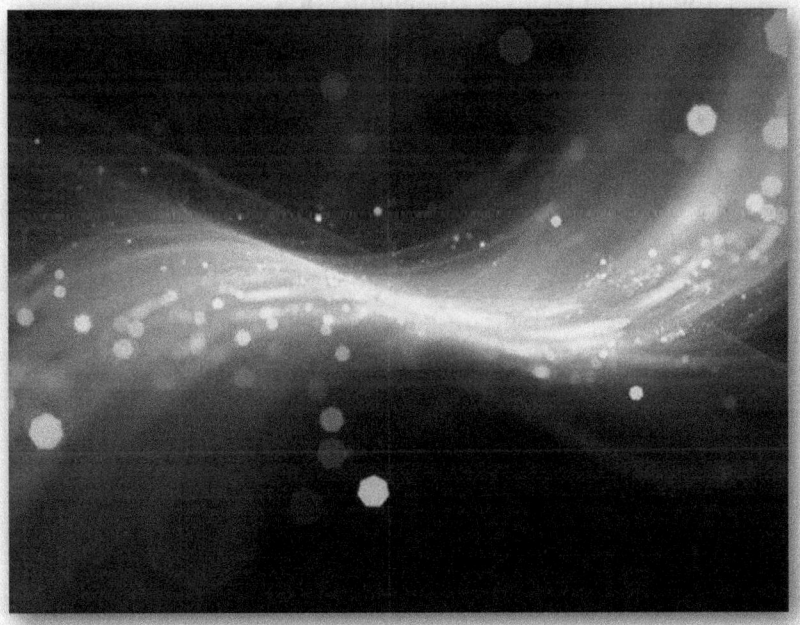

Mirroring begins to happen naturally with practice. You'll be able to feel that the rhythm is good, that things feel natural, and that there's a natural flow to your conversation as you hit the same frequency as the customer. Mirroring is like a duet.

The most important thing you can learn about mirroring is to *remember* it and that at first, you need to remind yourself to do it. When you do it the right way, the positive impact is undeniable.

When you have mastered mirroring, it's fine to just be yourself as long as you always lean toward mirroring. It's like learning to bicycle. You will feel the balance eventually. You just have to practice it over and over again.

The elements of mirroring

Informal and formal styles of communication

People are usually *formal* or *informal* in their styles of communication.

- Listen to whether the person you are talking to is using a broader accent and has certain "curves" in his or her tonality—this is typical of those who live in more rural areas. These are typically *informal* people. While remaining professional, be more broad and informal in your delivery. Simplify it, but don't talk down to the person as if he or she were not smart.
- If the person appears more *formal*, as though he or she lives in a city, you should use the same type of language with a more proper tone. Try to be firm and clear in your speech while still being engaging and conveying enthusiasm in a self-controlled manner.

The level of formality should be something you are able to sense. You should be able to feel whether you're going in an informal or formal direction. Of course, how informal or formal you can be depends upon the level of formality in your sales environment.

Volume

The volume of your voice should always be clear and assertive, but it should also vary to adapt to the volume of the customer's voice. You can lower the volume slightly for those who speak softly, but speak louder to those who do likewise. Generally, the volume of your voice should be normal, or slightly higher, and should always be clear. A self-confident person generally speaks a little louder in a room, but not in a forced way. Aim to speak at a volume that is a little bit louder than normal, something in between normal and slightly louder.

Vocabulary

Use their words.

When you have listened to them talk, you can use the same words or phrases they used earlier. Don't overdo this, but know that people express themselves in specific ways and use specific words and phrases and that those words and phrases mean something special to them.

Words don't mean the same thing to all people. People associate different things with them.

When you use their words later on, they will feel that you understand them better. It can be beneficial to tap into their vocabularies sometimes. Still, you have to be yourself.

Words can hold different meanings for people, so there might be reasons why they use specific words. This also applies to sentence structure and the way people say things, not only the words.

Similarity creates connection and trust and helps them understand what you are saying a lot easier.

Pace

Vary the pace and speed of your speech. Try to match the pace of customers. They are used to the ways they talk because that's how they talk to themselves in their heads, and that's also how they like to receive information. Some people speak extremely fast, while others speak more slowly. So adjust your speed to their preferred paces.

Meanwhile, focus on speaking clearly whenever you do speed up. When people talk very slowly, be a tiny bit faster than they are, because they may like to listen to speech that is slightly faster than their own. If they tend to speak very slowly, they may simply be tired.

Be them

Imagine that you are them, and pretend that you are saying what they would have said. Simply put, imagine that you are them. *Be them, and say exactly what they would have said.* I repeat this because it's the only way I can explain it, and I know this strategy is highly effective in increasing the number of calls you convert into sales. A few people may seem impossible to sell to, but the very same people might be easy to sell to if you tailor your conversation to them as though you were them.

People particularly like to talk with others who remind them of themselves. As you talk to them, they'll think, "Oh, I also like this thing," "I agree," "That's absolutely right," and "Oh, this person is like me; this person gets me."

On a subconscious level, this will make them feel safe and confident because they will feel as if you were another part of themselves.

Last note on this: Mirroring is powerful and is very beneficial in sales, but it should be used in moderation in relationships. It's far better for you to be yourself so that the people you are with know how to relate to you. It's nice to mirror somewhat, but in order for other people to relate to you, you have to be yourself completely and just allow some mirroring to happen naturally.

We live this life now and don't know what happens afterward, so be you—now. When you tell others what you like, your life will be much better. Perhaps you mistakenly think that the other person likes video games, but he or she actually doesn't; then you will both talking about something you are not interested in.

Being yourself feels great. Also, this point is not to mean that you should avoid seeing similarities and being agreeable, because you absolutely should do that. Seeing other people's perspectives and seeking to feel what they feel is a natural part of connecting.

Vocal Techniques.

Make your voice fascinating to listen to. Some people can talk about anything, and it still sounds like the most fascinating thing you have ever heard, as you cling to every word and want to hear what happens next. The voices of these people generate feelings in your body comparable to the way a roller coaster does. They go fast, slow, up, and down, and you just feel as if you have to pay attention.

Try saying something in an ordinary way, and then say it as if it were the most groundbreaking discovery you have figured out.

Of course, not everything you say has to sound like a groundbreaking discovery, but you will get a sense of how your tonality can be changed. There are other good tonalities, like a warm tone, a happy tone, a friendly tone, and so on.

To speak in an interesting way, your own tone should vary.

In general, you should speak in a determined manner. Speak in a confident and giving tone rather than one that seeks approval. Of course, you have nothing to seek approval for. You are simply in the conversation to spread positive energy and give.

1. VARIATION.

The most important objective of your tone of voice is to convey a genuine interest in what you're talking about. So first and foremost, be interested in what you're talking about. Why is the topic fascinating? What are the benefits of what you're saying? Why is it important?

Again, this brings us back to the concept of *being* instead of *acting*. There is more power in focusing on *where* the words come from rather than *how* you say them. So mentally programming yourself to increase interest in what you are talking about is more powerful than the technical focus on how you say the words. Still, the technical knowledge can make your tonality even better, but that has to happen after you have programmed yourself mentally.

After you master this principle, you can talk about anything. Anything you say will come to life. It's the opposite of a monotonous voice.

The main principle that creates an interesting tone of voice is variety. Try to talk with a varied tone of voice, add *power behind specific* words, and put some extra emphasis behind certain syllables.

Orchestras and artists use many different tones, volumes, paces, pressures, and rhythms. Choose to be an orchestra rather than someone reading the lottery numbers out loud.

You can try saying a word with the same feeling that the word represents. Try saying these words with different feelings: *Heart* (heartfelt). *Strong. Solid. Eternal. Boulder. Together.* Then try other words. Try to make the words sound like what they stand for.

When you talk about something with feeling, customers will feel that the product really is "solid" when you say that word with emotion. Try adding body language that represents what the word stands for as well.

Your feelings toward your product will also impact the way you say the name of your product.

> *Speak LOUDLY and clearly, and add the qualities*
> *of calmness, empathy, and thoughtfulness.*

You should also intend to convey a general attitude with your voice, such as happiness, determination, empathy, professionalism—or, better yet, a combination of all these.

Remember to vary your tempo, vary your tone, take pauses—and use power behind certain words. You'll soon notice how everything suddenly seems *much* more interesting. Being very enthusiastic at certain points in the conversation is good, but always stay self-controlled. Think of a boiling kettle that almost boils over.

Intentionally make everything you say come alive. Try saying a sentence in a dull, monotonous tone of voice. Then say the same sentence with great variation in how you say it.

Beyond the technical components, emotions dictate the tone of voice you will end up with. Therefore, amplify emotions within yourself to fascinate the people you talk to. Immerse yourself in what you say.

2. Assertiveness.

The most assertive person in the conversation will have the most impact. You must be the leader of the conversation and steer it toward improving the life of the customer.

Your tone should mimic a varied curve that goes up and down as you speak and then ends in a downward turn. Sloping downward toward the end of the sentence illustrates assertiveness. You shouldn't seek the customer's acceptance. Add stress at the beginning of the sentence rather than at the end. This small tweak can make a big difference.

Nonassertive	Assertive
What would you LIKE? Is that all right with YOU?	So WHAT would you like? IS that all right with you?

Add stress at the beginning of the sentence.

The assertiveness in your tone of voice is first and foremost dictated by how assertive you feel. You know that you're benefiting the customer. You are the leader. You are in control of the conversation. You are confident that the product is high quality. You are skilled, and the customer wants this.

Tone of agreement

When you have what I call a tone of agreement, you talk as if you and the customer are in agreement with each other. Think about the tone of someone who agrees very much with another person, and use that tone. If you say a sentence while nodding your head, you will feel this tonality. Go in this direction when speaking to your customers, and remember that you are a team.

CHAPTER 8

How You Can Shape the Future of Your Sales Career.

* * *

SALES TRAINING.

SELLING CAN BE LEARNED.

You can learn everything you need to become an ideal sales consultant. You simply have to integrate all the necessary pieces. Each piece of the puzzle will help you see a bit more of the full picture and give you more success.

> *A problem cannot be solved at the same level of thinking with which it was created.*
>
> —ALBERT EINSTEIN

You will have to think for yourself and take massive action while constantly learning from others and progressing toward your true sales greatness.

The benefits of learning about sales are that you will eventually be able to work the same amount of time while earning twice or five times as much money as previously. The time you put into practicing and preparing will be returned to you a hundred times.

If you read 1 hour every day for a week and learn something essential that lets you close twice as many sales, then you'll earn twice as much that month.

Instead of working two months, you can work one month and earn the same amount. Those 7 hours you spent learning was enough to give you back twenty additional workdays within that month. That means you got back 160 hours of productive work.

But that's not all. Your increased skills and knowledge will be applied in the future too, which means you'll get an extra year of productive work, 2,000 additional hours, for each year you work. In five years' time, this will correspond to 10,000 additional hours worked compared to how much you would have earned if you hadn't spent those initial hours expanding your knowledge and expertise.

So the 7 hours it took to learn something that doubled your income gave you back an additional 10,000 hours in five years and 100,000 hours in fifty years. This is the power of learning and increasing your sales per hour.

Doubling your income is smart. Let's say it took you 60 hours instead of 7 hours to double your income by listening to sales training every day for one to two months. This time investment would still be worth it. You'll get such tremendous value from learning every day.

You are reading this book, so I know that you understand the tremendous importance of learning.

Some people just do not grasp how much they'll get back by learning about sales, performing better, and expanding their knowledge about their products. They think that the extra hour they could spend learning should be spent doing something else instead. They don't consider the fact that they could be twice as great a salesperson, earn more, and have more freedom.

In fact, if you remain dedicated to learning and expanding your skills, you'll most likely earn more than just twice the amount you earn today. You will probably double it again and again. There is no limit to your income, and there have to be people on all income levels.

If you listen to sales training or self-improvement material every day, you will quadruple your earnings, at least. Promotions will open up, new opportunities will appear, and you will realize your greatness.

Here is a simple recipe for success:

1. Listen to self-improvement and sales training at least one hour each day. Some top performers listen to sales training for two, three, or four hours every day. If you can remain committed to at least two hours every day, though, that is great.

2. Read about your product for a minimum of thirty minutes a day until you know everything. After that, continue to learn regularly about your product.

3. Work enthusiastically, and keep going no matter what until you achieve your goals.
4. Think. Write down what works in an expensive book. Purchase a notebook that costs a little more than normal, and treasure the ideas you record in it.

When you get into the flow of doing these things every day, everything will become much easier. Society is designed to reward smart-working people who perform well exponentially more than average workers. Your goal is to be the best that you can possibly be as fast as possible, so you can make your dreams come true and help people along the way.

Of Course the Customer Is Receiving Your Product.

This part is absolutely *central* to your quest to become a top salesperson. Of course they are going to buy. It's critically important to know that before you even begin the conversation with clients, they should already have received your product. Of course they are going to get your product; you are simply delivering it to them.

It goes without saying that they simply must have your product. It's obvious. It's a great product, the delivery is good, it's easy to understand, and it offers so many benefits to customers. Assume that they must have it. Customers will then naturally think they should have it—you're only there to help and to give it to them.

Mastering this mind-set makes your job much more fun and easy. The basis of your conversation should be that customers' intent to buy is self-evident. All you need to do is tell them a little bit about the product and how they will receive and use it, and check that you have their correct addresses before the product is shipped.

This mind-set shines through in the tone of voice you use, your attitude, and your implementation of strong language.

Always use strong words in your conversation with customers, and present your product in a positive way. For example, your product is "tremendously" good, and customers have been "allowed to receive" two months' worth of your product. You don't need to say, "You have been allowed to receive this," but it's an example of a phrase that shows the correct attitude to have. You are the giver, and it's self-evident that they are going to enjoy this.

This is a lot better than saying your product is "actually quite good" or asking customers whether they'd "maybe like to try it." The product *is* good. That's why you're giving it to them. And you are calling to inform

The customers have never talked to you before, so when the conversation begins, they are waiting to see what you believe will happen. Therefore, you decide that they are obviously going to buy. What you believe, they believe.

Humans have social antennae that pick up on how others expect them to behave. Most people are very influenced by this, and even those who know about this force are still influenced by it to some degree.

So if someone comes along and is 100 percent confident that you should have his or her product and that it is the best thing for you, you will subconsciously begin to believe it yourself. Because this technique requires a level of product enthusiasm that is hard to fake, those who manage to act this way often really do have a great product. So when you have this energy of obviousness, this makes the customer believe this must be a great product.

People love professionals who offer a solution they can lean on.

People have become more self-reliant these days, but they still want to be led. If someone comes into your life as a friendly, professional, enthusiastic, fun-to-talk-to person that you know will help you, you'll feel comfortable with being helped.

Take the sale as self-evident. If your product is good, of course customers are going to say yes. This is the reason why it can sound so easy when you listen to true masters of selling sell. They have the tonality of obviousness.

This principle gives you the ability to reach even higher levels in sales—when you stop trying and start expecting.

Re-Gear.

Re-gearing is the same as resetting yourself. I just like the word "re-gearing" better because it provides a completely different feeling and makes me envision something else. I envision shifting gears to get more power.

When talking about re-gearing, keep in mind that the responses of customers can be very different. For example, if you call on a win-back list to try to win back customers who previously canceled a subscription, one reason for their cancelations may be simply that they stockpiled too many packages but were otherwise satisfied. Some might have been travelling for a year and been forced to cancel, and some may have had a rare, unfortunate experience with the product or customer service. In these cases, when you call again, the responses you receive can vary greatly. But don't allow customers to shift your gears. Always be in a peak state.

Think positively when you make the call, because you may suddenly come across three customers in a row who were all happy with your product and really want it, and want to buy a lot. You have to be ready at all times.

Keep in mind that you are constantly shaping the behavior of customers, and they will react completely differently to you depending on whether you are doing things right. Nevertheless, it may be helpful to keep in mind that people have different reasons for their actions.

On a win-back list, you should repeat to yourself over and over again that customers simply had a few too many packages but were still happy with the product. They just needed to stop for a while. This will help you have the most positive expectations for each conversation, which the customer will attune to.

Always expect everyone to want your product, and if you do end up closing this sale, be ready for the next one. Be positive all the time, and re-gear when you need to. If you manage to stay high on the positivity scale more often than other sales consultants, you are more likely to sell more than they do. The law of averages works all the time, and you have to make sure the general possibility of a sale is as high as it can be all the time. Tell yourself that the next conversation is going to be a sale, guaranteed.

Re-gearing gives you a power that few sales consultants have, one that will, in turn, increase your profits. It gives you the power to enter optimal performance in an instant.

Re-gearing is great. By re-gearing, you are almost guaranteed to have a great day every day because you will have control over your state. Others will look to you for strength when you do this.

The key to re-gearing is to abruptly snap right back into the zone in an instant. Re-gearing is a response to a voice in your head that says, "You should re-gear now," and then you immediately do it. There is *such* power in this. If you don't do this, too much time can go by between optimal performances. Think about the *huge* difference when you re-gear immediately every time you need to. You will be in an optimal state for a larger part of the day.

The power lies in the moment to snap right back into optimal performance.

When I need to re-gear, I get up, clap my hands, say "Re-gear!" to myself, and think, "OK, let's go!" The next call will be a sale.

If I am not in an optimal state, I suddenly notice it and think, "I'm not operating optimally right now." I clap my hands and think, "Let's go!" Now I'm optimal again.

This habit allows me to instantly put myself in the right gear again. If you make a habit of switching gears when you need to, your next call will always go very well—even if the last one didn't.

Think about those periods when you are in the zone. Many people find themselves in the zone and perform well for a time but don't reenter the zone quick enough if needed. This is not how it should be.

Activate the zone, be productive, and be the best version of yourself, and if for whatever reason you're not in the zone, clap your hands (or trigger yourself in whatever way you want) and jump right back in.

Can you imagine being in the zone *all* the time?

Moving your body is a great way to anchor the psychological re-gear.

Switching gears several times during the day will keep you on your toes and allow you to remain in your top mental gear for the majority of the day. Live in this state all day, all week, all month, and forever, and you will be amazed about at you can achieve.

This is the power of machines. With plenty of energy, they just keep going.

Re-gear into the zone immediately. Stay there, and enjoy it.

Efficiency.

The more calls you create time for, the more sales you will be able to close.

Talk *only* about what's important. By this, I mean that you should talk to customers only about things that give them value. Remember you will *double* your sales if you cut in half the time you spend on each call.

However, you must also make customers feel as if you were taking your time with them. You have to give them a detailed presentation, but say only what's important. The result will be a well-balanced and effective presentation.

Remember to talk only about what gives the customer value. This principle especially applies to mass sales, in which case you will have to refine your approach. Remove all unnecessary material, and leave only your top stuff. It's like having a nugget of gold covered in dirt. You don't need the dirt. Wipe it off, and present only the gold.

Let's say you ordinarily spend ten minutes on a call, but using the strategies above, you could shorten this time to five minutes. You will then have five extra minutes to make a new call that could lead to a sale. So you can double your sales by being efficient. If you can make a sale in shorter time period, that is better.

You can also refine your approach for the more time-consuming sales as well. Whatever you feel doesn't add any actual value should not be included in your sales pitch. If it doesn't increase buying temperature, it isn't needed, unless it provides value to the pitch by creating structure to your presentation.

Refining your approach in this way will also increase the overall value of your pitch. Five minutes of top material is better than ten minutes of suboptimal material with some of your top material sprinkled in. A five-minute presentation of top material ensures that the incentive to buy only increases. (Again, you have to make the pitch long enough to influence the customer, but some sales are actually this length.)

Customers like to be able to digest the material, and they require a certain amount of information regarding your product. You know how much is needed.

Focus on the gold, and keep everything else nice and simple. You'll get more calls in less time, and customers will see greater value in your presentation.

The speed of the call is determined not by how much you rush but rather simply by what you prioritize. You don't need to summarize the entire history of the company and yourself. Customers care only about whether the product will provide them the specific benefits they're interested in. This is the only thing that matters. You can use yourself as an example if you have had personal experiences with the product, but the focus should be on benefits.

> *Customers care only about whether the product will provide them the specific benefits they're interested in.*

You experience a very special feeling when you reach peak efficiency. Think about feeling very calm while, at the same time, completing productive task after productive task. This is the feeling athletes experience when they are being optimally efficient, running as fast as they can, and completing very intricate tasks, all while simultaneously having a unique calmness about them.

> *Be fast, but don't hurry!*
>
> —John Wooden

Make the Customer Feel Great.

Make the customer feel as good as possible in as many ways as possible.

Always praise customers, act impressed, and make them feel good about themselves. These actions will add value to the overall transaction. Customers pay to feel good; that is the reason they buy anything. You'll increase your own perceived value (as well as the product's perceived value) by making them feel good about themselves and as though they are great people.

Sales is all about helping customers feel and recognize that the value of your product is higher than the price. And since you are talking about and delivering the product, you are a part of the product yourself. You, therefore, increase the value of your product by increasing your own value. The best way to increase your own value is to develop yourself and make customers feel good about themselves. And if you encourage customers to feel good about themselves, they will be more willing to listen to you—and listen more closely—since you're obviously a great judge of character.

The best way to get others interested in what you're telling them is to first be interested in them and what they're saying. Customers will automatically draw the subconscious conclusion that your interest in them indicates that you have common interests and that they should also be interested in your product, since you're interested in the same things as they are.

All people like it when others are impressed with them or find them interesting. Try to genuinely be interested in customers—it's intriguing how people have different mind-sets and view the world differently.

Go the Extra Mile.

The people who stand out the most are the ones willing to go that extra mile. Always go the extra mile whenever the opportunity presents itself. Work a little longer, and show up to work a little earlier. Put a little bit more effort into every conversation.

Ask for the sale one more time. Give an extra compliment if the customer deserves it. Be your best self in whatever you do. If needed, spend a bit more time helping out the customer. All these little things add up.

> **Be the best version of yourself in anything you do.**
>
> —Stephen Curry

When you adopt this golden principle, customers can sense that you're putting in that extra effort. As a result, they will open up a bit more and allow you to give them even more of your product. The trick to following this principle is to ask yourself this question:

WHAT ARE THE STANDARDS OF THIS JOB?.

When you are aware of the general standards, you can then create your own standards and expectations. If your job starts at eight thirty, try to be there at eight fifteen or earlier if possible. And be completely ready once you get there. If customers expect to be treated a certain way, then surpass those expectations by treating them especially well.

In all honesty, optimal performance is all it takes. Who sets the standards at your job? You might as well improve upon these standards by implementing and following your own. This way, you'll always be going the extra mile and constantly performing optimally. In my experience, this appears to inspire some mystical, magical component to work for you as well, as if the universe somehow rewards you for your extra effort.

Focus on the Positive Things.

Unless an episode with a negative customer was particularly funny, talk only about the yes customers with your colleagues.

Talk only about the positive things that happen. Everything you say should increase your PMA and the PMAs of those around you.

Talk only about and focus only on what you want to have happen. You should challenge yourself to intelligently select the words you use. If you must say something that is not positive, say it in a positive or constructive way. Declare, for example, that someone should have more energy instead of saying he or she is tired or lazy.

Connection.

Connection occurs when we see ourselves in others. When you talk to a customer about something that you both care about, you create a connection. If you both care about football and talk about that, a connection will be made. Connections are quickly created by finding common denominators. Connections are strengthened even further when your personalities and energies are synchronized. Connections develop in the moments when a customer thinks, "I agree!" about something you've said. The trick to creating connections is to think about and predict what customers care about, and then present these things to them as if you were them yourself.

Thinking that you are already friends with the customer and focusing on inspiring that friendly energy is another way to increase connections. This mindset creates a tone of voice that generates a feeling of connection. However, this should be done in a natural way. If the customer is an older person, you should refrain, of course, from referring to him or her as "buddy," and so forth. The idea is to allow your tone of voice to reinforce familiarity between you and the customer.

You should also keep in mind that you are on the same team as your customer, because you are. After all, you're calling to help the customer.

Create Attention..

Your customers were likely engaged in something entirely different before you contacted them. But once you're on the phone with them or talking to them, you should aim to be their only focus.

Your intro should tap into the value you're bringing them, and you should come across as a natural, professional, happy, and overall all right person. Feel free to be enthusiastic if you feel like it.

Be yourself. You are a great person, and they're lucky to be talking to you—plus, the only reason you're calling is to make their lives better. So create a smart intro that focuses on value and grabs the customer's attention.

In the intro, you should be professional and orderly while still showing happiness and being energetic and self-controlled. At the intro stage, some sales environments require a higher energy output, while others require a more self-controlled output of energy. You can still have energy and oomph behind what you're saying. Steve Jobs was a master at letting enthusiasm seep through everything he said while at the same time being completely self-controlled.

Try to encourage customers to say yes as early as possible, and also say something that really grabs their attention. Tell them the benefits of the product as early as possible. Throw in some positive information, and let customers feel that this conversation is important, valuable, and easy. In modern sales, it's important not to come across as a stereotypical salesperson. Instead, be natural and talk to customers as if you know them. Then you won't trigger any red flags.

Naturalness is a key part of the intro. Having energy is a must, but you must also adjust the pressure of your intro according to what you're selling.

Befriending the Customer.

Befriending customers always has a positive effect. Friendship creates great value in and of itself, and if they have any interest in the product to begin with, it will increase the likelihood of customers buying. Inspiring a friendship with customers will create an additional positive element within the sale and product for customers to take into consideration. Everyone values the opinions of his or her friends, and customers might feel more inclined to buy your product just because you are a friend.

Friendships between salespeople and customers also create more loyalty to the product. All you need to do is get in touch with customers, be positive, talk about common interests, and make customers feel good. Think about all the ways you can help customers feel good about themselves.

If a friend offers you something, you know you would be more inclined to buy it simply because you are a friend. Friendship is just one more principle that adds up to the total value you offer, and it is also a powerful force that boosts repeat sales, referrals, and up-sells.

GUTS.

The fun thing about selling is that you get to meet so many people.

To have successful interactions, your guts should be optimal all the time. Guts is about giving your all every time, putting yourself fully out there, and simply being all you can be. You become gutsy by understanding that while you live here, you might as well give it your all.

There is another essential element to becoming gutsy. If you understand this element, you will be gutsy all the time. You may already know it, but you have to remember it, and it is that sometimes we just don't know why people do what they do.

In sales, you learn about all the behaviors and thought processes of people. So to a certain degree, you should always know why customers do what they do. But every now and then, you'll come across a customer you just cannot understand or who is acting in a funny way. In this case, it's important to remember that you can never know *everything* about why people behave the way they do.

You may know enough to help that person make the right choice and have a good interaction, but you can't understand everything. Sometimes a customer will just react in a completely unexpected way.

Think about the times when you didn't know the reason for why a person did what he or she did, and you didn't find out the reason behind this behavior until long after. Therefore, you should never take anything in sales personally or be affected by it. This is how we can define compassion: proactively seeking to understand the other person. Ask questions if the customer does something odd, to understand the customer better. If you don't have time to ask more questions, simply realize that sometimes we don't know the whole life story of the other person. By remembering this, we are given the freedom to keep our guts high all the time and never care how anyone else thinks or reacts. The only thing that matters is that you learn more and more, give your all, and are kind.

If you do that, greatness will follow.

With this understanding and compassion toward people, you will always continue on and be optimal because you are the deciding force that determines how you feel.

CHAPTER 9

Body Language and Adding Value to Your Product by Being Your Best Self.

* * *

Body Language.

Lean forward, stand up, have good posture, make gestures, and move throughout the day.

These tips are based on the idea that motion creates emotion and that your body language affects how you feel. You'll always feel better by raising your chest, having open body language, and holding your shoulders back while moving. It's common sense, but it might be a good idea to remind yourself of these things over and over again. It's also very important to lean forward a little bit and show attention, especially if you are selling through the phone. Your body language affects your state of mind.

For telemarketing: Know that your body language is heard over the phone and affects your tone of voice, energy, and mind-set.

For sales in person: Learn about and master body language.

1. Your body language should be confident, open, friendly, and professional. Imagine that you are the customer when you mirror, but have slightly better body language than they have if they don't

have good body language. The best body language stems from your intentions. If you're ready to help the customer and have the energy and enthusiasm to do so, then your body language will be great and welcoming. If you talk to people and have fun throughout the day, this positivity will inevitably affect your body language. Positive thoughts are also highly important for great body language.
2. There are exercises that you can do to strengthen your back and stretch out your chest. Just try searching for "posture exercises" on the Internet.

PHYSICAL ELEMENTS TO REMEMBER:.

- Keep your shoulders back and down.
- Keep your chest up (in a natural way).
- All eye contact should be natural. Keep eye contact, but remember not to stare your customer down. Look away every now and then to make it comfortable and keep things natural.
- Smile in as natural and genuine a manner as possible and as often as possible. This is done by amplifying things that make you happy within your mind and deciding to be happy.
- Have fun and enjoy yourself.
- Keep your arms and hands open.
- Nod in a natural way every now and then to show that you agree.
- Make gestures in a way that feels genuine and comfortable in order to create images and enthusiasm about what you're talking about.

There's no need to overthink your body language, but it's useful to learn these tips because they have the potential to make you more influential.

A simple touch on the shoulder and a firm handshake can also have a lasting effect on the customer. Here, you'll need to find a balance for each customer according to how he or she likes to communicate. Some people communicate in a more physical manner than others.

1. Your posture should be upright and professional while still remaining loose.
2. Now it's time to mirror the customer. Begin by keeping your mirroring low key. One expert tip is to mirror the breathing of the other person. Breathing at the same rate as the customer can provide a powerful boost for creating a deep connection. He or she will not notice it as long as you do it in a natural way—by not holding your breath and not counting your breathing rate on your fingers to time your exhales perfectly.

You'll notice pretty quickly how the other person uses his body language to communicate. Mirroring the body language of the other person will open up the channels of communication even more.

You can also use pacing and leading here. When you have mirrored customers naturally for a while, it will be easier to lead them afterward.

Pacing = mirroring

Leading = to lead your customers toward something that is beneficial for them

When you are selling to someone, you also have the ability to send them positive energy. As you focus on having great body language, you can also focus on sending very positive energy to the customer. You send this energy subconsciously by intending to do it, and it will express itself in your tonality, word selection, and body language. This will make your body language better automatically.

There is another reason for why this is powerful too. This reason is that people can feel what you feel. So spend time on making yourself feel great away from your work, and you'll reap the benefits when you are working. People can sense it when you love yourself, love life, and feel great about all the progress you're making. This energy will come through to your customers in your conversations with them.

All the positive things you do to develop yourself as a person make you more influential to your customers.

Habits.

Begin your day strong. Habits are the building blocks of our lives.

Eating a healthy breakfast, doing your morning ritual, and entering the zone early will have a massive impact on your day; this momentum will pile up and make a big difference by the end of the month.

You are going to have to enter the zone each day eventually, so why not enter it as early as possible? I tell you, when you enter flow several days in a row, you can wake up smiling and saying, "Let's go!" as you eagerly look forward to optimizing the day.

Everything you can do to contribute to your success can be made into a habit. Habits are simply things that we *usually* do. We have willpower, and with willpower, we can shape our habits.

The more often you do something, the less energy it requires. So use all your willpower to create optimally positive habits, and then these new habits will gradually become completely normal to you, allowing you to work hard all the time. Working hard will actually become easy. You will actually find it easier to work hard than not to, because working hard will be normal.

Habits are like streams of water; the more they flow in a certain direction, the deeper they dig, becoming stronger and larger. But if you use your willpower to dig a new pathway that is more optimal and leads in a different direction, eventually the water will begin to naturally flow along this new pathway.

The more your brain utilizes a specific brain pathway, the more the new pathway is strengthened. So when the brain chooses which way to go, fueled by willpower, it will choose the right way. Eventually the old pathway will become weaker, and the new pathway will become dominant and your default. So willpower is one thing that can shape your habits.

Another thing that can powerfully change your habits is creating new links in your brain. When you make new connections, you can also effortlessly create new pathways. For example, if you understand how truly beneficial it is to learn, you will begin to spend time learning, even though the pathway created to make you learn is fairly new. This is because the pathway in your brain has been connected in a more efficient way by linking the desired outcome with that specific activity: learning. So you link learning with the rewards of achieving specific outcomes, whereas previously your brain might have linked learning to homework or something boring. So when you create a new connection, it is changed forever, and you don't need willpower.

Creating success is essentially about selecting which habits you want to form and using willpower plus understanding to form new and better pathways. When all your habits align to help you become a great salesperson, selling becomes effortless. This is actually how it should be. Many of us have not been surrounded by top performers, and so we haven't formed efficient links. Today, you can now expose yourself to the right people through books or in person, and this makes it even easier to form habits.

Forming habits really is easy, but we've all been told the myth that it is too hard. While it can be challenging at times, habit formation is actually much easier than people think.

> *Our culture teaches us that making significant change takes a long time and is difficult to do. This is simply NOT true. Change happens in an instant. It is not a process—it is something you do in an instant by simply making a decision.*
>
> —Tony Robbins

Momentum also ties into habits. You create momentum by doing more and more right things and doing them in more efficient ways, which accelerates progress even further. One change will make other changes easier. These great habits will keep stacking up as you progress, increasing your momentum. Everything affects everything. Eating, sleeping, learning, achieving, training, being kind, and so on all affect one another.

Imagine an NBA basketball player who learns how to dribble so well that he doesn't have to look down at the ball anymore and can instead look up and focus on scoring. Once the player has mastered this, he can use his energy to plan and strategize while playing. At the next level, he can start thinking about how best to lead his team and organize the team in a way that will end in victory.

Let's say he continues to practice shooting, strength training, running, and technical drills. These skills will eventually become second nature. They will all collect into one great accumulation of basketball skills. All great people continue to perform optimally because they have their own standards. Their standards are how it should be. So they are not overperforming; they are performing only in accordance with their standards. Eventually, by continuing this way, you can become an entity as powerful and determined as Stephen Curry, who constantly flies from zone to zone and operates at an extremely high level.

The next level of thinking that Stephen Curry operates from is to think about the strengths and weaknesses of the individuals on each team. He doesn't even have to think about the other skills that he's already mastered, like dribbling, because these skills are simply habits now. It would be very interesting to know what he thinks about. He probably focuses most on the feel of the game, energies, and some strategy. Perhaps he relies heavily on instinct.

Great sales consultants make skills second nature and raise their awareness to higher focuses, like energies, what type of personality the customer has, and so on. The great sales consultants also begin to listen to their intuition and operate behind all the words being said.

At this point, your enthusiasm, professionalism, and empathy have already become so natural that these principles are operating on autopilot.

You'll free up more energy with each habit you establish as second nature, since habits are easy to perform. This free energy can then be used to create new, efficient habits and optimize additional principles. Habits are so powerful that basketball players sometimes have problems missing a basket on purpose because they automatically shoot to score.

There are many habits for you to create. Putting yourself in the zone is one of these habits, as is doing it as early as possible in the day.

Other habits could include telling yourself how much you like yourself, your job, and your life over and over again. You can also adopt more-specific habits, like competing with yourself until lunch.

The positive habits will then become your standard of normalcy, and you'll become a so-called constant top performer. Focusing on optimizing your habits is powerful.

Your standards will become higher as your principles evolve and you attempt to constantly maximize your progress. Once habits begin to propel you forward in life and you use willpower in the same direction, your progress will accelerate more and more.

Be aware of your own autopilot, and optimize this autopilot. Habits determine your life's quality.

THERE ARE TWO PRIMARY WAYS OF FORMING HABITS, AND THEN SOME ADDITIONAL ONES:.

1. Learn more and understand more so that new connections are made in your brain.

New information can cause permanent changes in your behavior. When you understand all the ramifications of something and decide that this is a more beneficial course of action, you will choose that course.

This is called focusing on your why. In inspirational teachings, instructors focus on bringing up all the reasons why you want to do something. I think this goes deeper. It's about creating a very streamlined pathway between certain actions and the results you want. When this connection is made, your brain will link the results to the action and make you take the connected action. Also, you will need to remove any unnecessary connections, if you have any, or create more-optimal connections.

For example, if you want to train and achieve a certain fitness result, you go through all the reasons why it will be beneficial to achieve that result. Then you say things to yourself like these:

- It really is easy to train. I only have to train three times a week for an hour if I'm aiming for strength gain anyway. That's nothing.
- Training actually feels good.
- I understand that training is not about pushing myself to failure all the time; it's actually better for strength gain to focus more on *activating* the muscles.
- It's better to do reverse pyramid training. (Search for that term.)

- In fact, I like to train; it's very natural for the body, as long as I understand I don't have to go to failure all the time. Then I can just enjoy training.
- Actually, pushing myself feels great.
- I love training. I get an endorphin and testosterone rush while I do it, and it makes me feel alive.
- Understanding that less is more is golden in training, and then I just give it my all.
- Every rep I do brings me closer and closer to achieving my goal, and that goal will give me this benefit, and that benefit, and that benefit, and so on.

You get a sense of how you are supposed to make efficient connections in your brain.

2. Use willpower to do something enough times until habit takes over.

3. Set up your life in a way that makes it natural to do certain things. A great example of this is to stock up your fridge and cabinets with healthy foods and healthy snacks so that the next time you go get some food, you make it inevitable to find healthy foods instead of unhealthy foods. Of course, you will need to remove the unhealthy snacks as well.

4. Visualize, listen to affirmations or incantations (affirmations said in an emotional way), create a vision board, and surround yourself with people who have those habits.

Use all these factors. The best one by far is the first one, and then the second one. Don't just understand; integrate the understandings completely, and create correct connections in your brain.

More and more optimal habits will be integrated into your personality and give you forward momentum as long as you continue doing the right things.

You Have Much More Power Than You Think!

Many people have untapped energy reserves. We actually have an infinite amount of energy, but we don't utilize anywhere near all the energy we have at our disposal.

In our childhoods, we have seen cartoon heroes in who were always able to find that last, necessary burst of energy when they needed it. We have seen other top people who are able to dedicate a huge amount of effort and truly give a task or problem everything they've got. If you simply try, then you'll be able to access even more power than you previously thought possible. If we try, we will always notice that we can create even more energy than what we already have.

This kind of extra energy is something that Muhammad Ali had plenty of and managed to access regularly in order to win boxing matches in the final rounds. He managed to access even more energy than his opponents for a longer period of time, and he was also just better overall.

My uncle once said, "We relax when we sleep." Of course, when you are pursuing your purpose and doing what you love, you are relaxed and having fun anyway. You should also recover in effective ways throughout the day.

Each time you use this power to close one more sale, you'll strengthen your faith in your own eternal energy resources even further. You may have seen someone run a long race and give everything he or she has got, and then, as he or she crosses the finish line, the winner will get an additional rush of dopamine, endorphins, and serotonin, raising his or her arms above his or her head and doing a victory lap, as if gaining renewed energy. As you achieve goal after goal, you gain renewed energy.

Keep in mind you have a lot more energy than you may think!

You've probably heard stories about mothers who have lifted cars to save their children, showing our true energy potential. Our potential is fascinating.

Discover how much productive effort you can really put forth, and you'll be amazed at the sales results you can generate. The victorious feeling afterward is also one of the best feelings in the world.

RECOVERY.

There's a fine line between giving everything you've got and giving too much. Among the population, 99.9 percent does not give enough, while some top performers give too much. Kobe Bryant, for example, gave too much throughout his career and slept too little, in my opinion. He even said this himself when he stated that he learned, as he grew older, to prioritize recovery a little more. Perhaps a little more recovery or sleep would have benefited him in terms of staying a little healthier. Recovery is very important.

You can focus on recovery by spending time with your friends, loved ones, and family and having fun with them.

Of course, life is much better if you're a top performer, because then you'll have more love, safety, friendship, joy, and ability to help others, and you'll just enjoy yourself more in general.

Our energy hormones are also affected by whether we stand or lie down. Energy hormones are calmed down when we lie down, so try to lie down with both legs up high during the day. Your body will recover and repair much more efficiently if your body is relaxed and your feet lean up against the wall. So remember to do a bit of repair and recovery every now and then so that you have more energy in the long run. Remember that overtime is not the answer. Learning and growing is the answer.

Sleep.

Sleep is important for life. Use all the willpower you have to *really* nail this habit. You *must* make a habit out of going to bed early and getting enough sleep. This will give you *much* more energy and improve your mood, memory, and creativity. You'll see things clearer, be more optimistic, and become stronger. Your immune system will also be stronger, and you'll handle situations a lot better. Sleep is crucial. It affects your whole life.

One comforting fact regarding sleep is that the hours you've slept during the last four days matter more than the hours you slept last night. So even if you haven't slept enough, you can perform perfectly well. But really, getting enough sleep will give you a huge advantage. All you need to do is make a habit out of it.

One day, even though I hadn't slept enough the night before, I was still able set a new personal sales record. The truth is that there are no excuses—you can do whatever you put your mind to, every day. I did, however, eventually set an even higher record on a day where I got plenty of sleep, and my weekly records are usually set when I implement the action steps to sleep well.

Children often want to stay up late because they can't really see how sleep is connected with their performance the next day. Some people also choose entertainment instead of goal attainment.

After you have set a new daily record, weekly record, or monthly record, you'll feel better than ever before, and you won't care at all about missing a few hours in front of the computer. The feeling of peace and bliss you get within yourself as you set a new record is truly magnificent.

Choose to have a happy life. You'll be so much more efficient when you go to bed early. Going to bed early is always the best investment you can make for yourself, so keep this in mind when deciding whether you should go to bed.

The general population does not get enough sleep, and they aren't living the life they want. But you are different—you are a winner. You want the best life possible for you. As long as you're also doing other things right, there are huge benefits to getting enough sleep.

Your quality of sleep is even more important.

HERE ARE ALL THE BENEFITS OF PLENTY OF SLEEP:.

- You feel better.
- More endorphins and serotonin are produced, and as a result, you become more relaxed while still feeling wide awake and energetic.
- You get a lot more done.
- You are much more positive, and you manifest the reality you want much more easily.
- You boost your immune system.
- You will close a lot more sales. This is a pattern I've consistently seen in sales. You will perform better overall because you have sustained energy all day.
- You become more alert and dialed in, and you think more clearly.
- You become more attractive, and your appearance improves.
- Your concentration and memory work better.
- You can learn up to 50 percent faster.
- In addition, you'll also be able to build more muscle and recover faster from training.

It feels amazing to be wide awake. People like people who radiate energy, focus, and joy. Your surroundings will become clearer than you've ever seen them before—as if you were experiencing a brand-new world. Your perception of the world will literally change depending on how well you've slept.

ACTION STEPS TO SLEEP BETTER.

- Make a habit out of going to bed early every day. This will become a habit if you stick with it for a few weeks.
- Cut caffeine intake completely after noon. This means no tea, Coca-Cola, coffee, or anything with caffeine. Better still, stop caffeine intake completely, and function on pure, natural energy all the time. If your adrenal glands (your energy-producing glands) are not optimized, you might have caffeine withdrawal, but you'll get over it.
- If you want to, consume soothing herbs at night, like lavender, lemongrass, chamomile, or other stronger herbs if needed, such as valerian or others.

- Purchase blue blocker glasses. These block blue light, which is believed to be the color of light that keeps us awake.
- Install f.lux on your computer, which is a computer program that blocks blue light on your devices.
- Dim the lights at night (or buy orange lightbulbs), or turn off as many lights as possible as early as possible, preferably right after the sun has set. By doing so, you'll get your melatonin production started earlier, leading to more total melatonin production at night, which means deeper sleep.
- Expose yourself to sunlight and bright light as soon as you wake up. This exposure turns off melatonin and begins production of serotonin and other wakefulness hormones.
- Make your room *completely* black, or use an eye mask.
- Your sleep bank will gradually build up. A good night's sleep helps, but getting four nights with plenty of sleep and a night with not much sleep is actually better than the opposite. When you have slept well five days in a row, you will recognize the energy building up. And when you have slept well for several months, you will achieve an even higher level of health because your body will have had more time to repair itself every day.

PUT YOURSELF IN THE SAME STATE OF MIND YOU WANT YOUR CUSTOMERS TO BE IN.

Raise your own buying temperature. In the same way that you can mirror others, customers will also subconsciously mirror you. This is because they have mirror neurons and can feel what you feel. They are also influenced by your actions and emotions. If you feel enthusiastic about buying the product and you're happy, these emotions will rub off on customers. The desire to buy should run in the background and have an indirect, positive effect on customers.

This is a typical NLP technique described as going first. (NLP is a set of principles that focus on how to influence people, among other things.) You must put yourself in the state you want the customer to be in, in order to make emotional osmosis work in your favor. Osmosis is a subtle, gradual absorption or mingling between two people. This means that the other person will gradually feel what you feel, to some degree. People can still choose their own feelings, but not many people are conscious of this.

The Science and the Art of Sales.

The beauty of sales is that it is both a science and, at the same time, an art form, full of creativity and inspiration.

There is a recipe for success in selling, a logical list of elements that should be included in a sales process.

Yet sales can also be viewed as an art form. You must be unique and creative and find your own unique way of selling that works best for you.

When you sell, you can enter a state of full flow, where you have a powerful influence on the customer and ooze charisma. Ingenious ideas will flow freely in the air and be turned into words that push the right buttons in the customer and have a seemingly magical effect.

Sales can be like a dance where you take elements you've already mastered and use them in your own way to best help the customer.

Say Things in a Way That Helps Customers Understand and Learn Something.

Provide customers with information, and let them associate it with something they recognize.

You can use sentences like this, for example:

"It's just like…"

"Think about…"

If you manage to explain slightly advanced knowledge and associate it with something they already comprehend, they will learn and understand.

When customers think (or say), "Oh! I get it!" that's gold. People like to understand things, and they also like to learn. As a result, the solution you present seems far more brilliant. You'll also appear to them as someone who knows what he or she is talking about, while still remaining relatable to each customer. Relate new knowledge to things they know about.

They're Buying the Feeling That You Represent.

When you feel great, customers will associate your positive emotions with your product. They'll subconsciously feel that if they purchase your product, then they will feel the same way that you do, to some degree. They'll wonder why you're feeling so good, and they'll begin to associate your good feelings with the product you represent.

Essentially, the customer buys whatever feeling you represent. You can get sales even if you don't feel good, but you'll definitely get better results the better you feel. When a customer buys, you will in turn feel even better about yourself.

All purchases are ultimately made based upon the feelings customers anticipate experiencing as a result of using your product.

Spread Joy.

Spread joy to those around you. The more positive energy you give to those around you, the more beneficial it will be for you as well. In sales, you benefit when other people do well, because their PMAs influence you positively.

Nevertheless, you must remember that everything is up to you, and you are fully responsible for your own results. No matter what other people do around you, you must still do the most optimal thing. You're competing only with yourself to achieve the highest-possible results.

Positive energy from others is a bonus, and it's a good idea to contribute to making the environment around you better. You will also like yourself even more when you do.

People have an intrinsic sense of justice, and we want things to be fair from the time that we are little children. As a result, we want to return the favor if someone does something nice for us. In other words, we might get something back in one way or another if we help other people. But it really doesn't matter whether we get anything back. The important thing is that we embody who we decide to be.

Being kind simply feels right. Giving is one of the most magical aspects of life. You probably remember the times you have helped your friends, your family, or even strangers. Remember how good that felt?

At the end of the day, the only things that matter are the results that we produce, that we're genuinely having fun, and that we're giving as much positive energy as possible.

You have to talk to people anyway, so why not decide to be a positive contributor to their lives? That's what will give your life meaning in the end. Tony Robbins once said, "I want to be a blessing in people's lives." Wow! Imagine how this mind-set has changed his life, how it has already made his life better, and how many other people have benefited from that mind-set so far.

Spreading joy is simply a matter of choosing the type of effect you have on others.

Happiness.

The underlying purpose of everything we do is ultimately to make ourselves and others happy. When you are happy, others see you as having value, because you have something other people want: happiness. Everyone wants to be happy. So when we see other people being happy, we subconsciously think they have something that can make us happy as well.

When you are happy, your brain is also more creative and functions better. You can, of course, perform well even if you're not particularly happy, but you'll definitely sell more if you're cheerful, happy, and joyous.

We have the responsibility to do what makes us happy.

This is your life.

We're efficient when we're happy. It's healthy to be happy, and other people become interested in us and we attract more good things when we decide to be happy. Many people who want to succeed and reach their goals don't think about using happiness as a tool to get there.

Another benefit of happiness is that you can make other people happy by sending them positive vibes, which in turn makes them more open to your ideas. Even if you don't say it, they will subconsciously think that your product makes people happy.

The energy of happiness should be combined with the energies of leadership, determination, fun, and giving. While you are happy, you should be in an active state in which you are engaged and steer the conversation in the direction that will most benefit the customer.

Smiling and laughing are great qualities in sales because they display charisma. They will soften up customers and open them up to receive your ideas.

Celebrating.

I am all *for* celebrating. You just have to celebrate.

As humans, we are like animals in that we are influenced by rewards. Every time you reach a goal, you should mentally or physically celebrate. This celebration will help your subconscious mind associate pleasure with taking the actions that make you reach your goals. Just put your hands in the air and cheer if you feel like it—it's natural. Plus, people around you will like it and allow themselves be more free.

You can also celebrate internally, if you prefer that.

Some people believe that celebrating will cause them to become too satisfied, sbut this is not true. You can celebrate your successes and use them to fuel new successes and immediately set a new goal.

You will make progress no matter what; the question is just whether you decide to feel good while you achieve your goals. Celebrating is actually *more* efficient in terms of making progress, because it makes the law of attraction work for you. The law of attraction states that we attract similar feelings to what we feel right now and actualize the thoughts we predominantly have.

CHAPTER 10

Build upon What Works.

* * *

Write It Down.

On days that you feel you are doing great, take time to write down what worked. Write down everything.

The success factors you discover may include being more professional, a specific phrase you used, how well you slept and ate, and your level of energy. Maybe you laughed and had fun with your colleagues while you were highly efficient.

Write down every success factor you can think of that you feel was important to you that day, and don't spare any details.

When you record the success factors you figure out, formulate them in your own unique way. When you write things your own way, you will understand the nuances of the success factors better, and they will be easier to remember. You can even make up new words for certain things, like "re-gearing," or for any other principle you come up with.

You can also rename other well-known principles, like hard work, closing, PMA, and so on. When you create your own names or formulate things in your own way, later it will be easier to enter those specific energies you are trying to describe and re-create them.

So if you think of hard work as smart work, that might create a different energy and attitude toward it. You could also write down that principle and phrase it in four additional ways:

- Being as efficient as possible
- Giving your all
- Simply being your true self
- Being the one who always does the most important action in the best way possible

You know what formulations will help you implement the principle in the best way. You might even write down more creative words to remember to be hardworking as well, such as "power machine" or something like that. Some phrasings have a better effect on your brain when you reread them or think about the principles.

Remember to continue doing what works. If you know what works, then do it again and again. That is one of the differences between the best salespeople and the mediocre ones. The best salespeople continue doing what's working and build upon those things.

Visualizing.

This is one of the biggest secrets among successful people that really isn't a secret at all.

All successful people have visualized living the lives they are now living. Before you can achieve something, you have to envision it. The more you envision it, the more you program your mind to realize it. Visualizing inspires you while at the same time connecting pleasure to a certain outcome, which in turn makes you automatically take more action. Visualizing also programs your subconscious mind to notice things in your environment that correspond to achieving that goal.

We have a filtration system in the brain called the reticular activating system (RAS). Essentially, this system filters out everything that isn't important and shows us what is important. Of course, we do have an instinct that helps us notice certain things and tries to help us, but the rest of the RAS is very flexible. There are millions of things to pay attention to, remember, and think about at every moment, so the RAS helps us focus on what's really important.

It turns out that what's important to us is based not just on instinct but also on what we have focused on previously and associated feelings with. When we attach emotions to something, like a specific car, we start seeing it everywhere because our RAS is tuned in to it.

You can consciously direct what your brain should focus on. In turn, your brain will then notify you when things within that focus show up in your thoughts or in your world. The RAS will actually illuminate previously unconsidered paths to achieving your goals, because your subconscious is constantly observing and storing huge amounts of information on your behalf. It's like talking to a genius who knows almost everything; you just need to tell the person what you want to know. In some ways, it's like a GPS that has stored tremendous amounts of data, and when you visualize, it's like typing in the address and the GPS forming a plan for the fastest way to get there.

When you have visualized a lot, you will automatically know the next steps to take.

We communicate with our subconscious minds by thinking about our goals and outcomes using pictures, sounds, and smells and associating these images with strong euphoric and happy feelings. Do this often, enjoy yourself, and really feel that you have already achieved your goal. Then you'll *really* put your subconscious to work, and it will inevitably show you the way to your goals. Suddenly, you will receive brilliant insight and inspiration, and you will feel where you should go next.

Our thoughts might very well be vibrations that attract circumstances in the universe or impact people around us, like radio waves. I don't honestly know whether our thoughts have any effect on the universe/multiverse around us, but sometimes it feels as if magic is actually happening when you visualize and your results suddenly appear.

Visualization gives you the confidence to do what you want to.

By the way, positive thoughts and visualizations are hundreds of times stronger than not-positive thoughts, so don't worry if not all your thoughts are positive; simply try your best to make them positive. As you consciously focus on great sales results, you create more of them. Visualizing your dreams is very fun.

In sales, visualization can be used to visualize your total amount of sales before lunch or throughout the day, week, month, or year. You can also visualize the dreams that go along with that sales greatness. The only way to reach your true dreams is to get better, and because of visualization, your brain will find a way to make your dreams become a reality.

With Customers on the Line.

When customers go back and forth trying to decide whether to buy, it is important to provide them reassurance. But it's even more important to increase their buying temperatures. These are two things you can do in such a scenario: reduce risk and increase desire.

Many people spend too much time reducing risk. It's better to briefly reduce perceived risk and effectively show the safety in receiving your product. This puts emphasis on just how obvious and safe it is.

After reassuring customers, you should focus on increasing buying temperatures even more to tilt them in the right direction so they feel that the product is worth more than any risk or sum of money. Immediately after assuring customers, you should flow naturally into focusing on benefits and help them to visualize and truly experience the positive benefits they'll receive from the product.

The desire to buy makes them less sensitive to the price of the product. If they want a product strongly enough, they'll buy it. Always focus on the benefits.

Always Agree with the Customer.

Always agree with the customer. The customer is always right. Listen to customers, see whether you agree with anything they're saying, and then use that as your foundation. If they say something, then say that you agree and speak with a tone of voice that genuinely expresses this agreement. Always try to create this feeling of agreement. In doing so, you'll be able to pull the conversation in the direction that you want, because they'll be on board.

No One Knows Anything.

One of the world's biggest secrets is that no one knows anything. People simply have different degrees of certainty in what *they* believe is true. We don't really know anything. We can be very certain of things, but that's all we can be. However, know that your product is great.

We learn by experiencing things for ourselves, listening to others, and then deciding what is true. We do not have time to experience absolutely everything for ourselves, and some things are simply not practical to experience.

So we have learned to use other people's knowledge, and we are affected by others' confidence in their beliefs and what they tell us. As a result, if you're selling a product that helps people, then be proud of it and say so in a determined and confident way. Know that you're giving them something that makes their lives better.

Of course, some things you can know are beneficial, such as doing good, being grateful, making progress toward your goals, being in the moment, and having fun. Those things are probably true.

CHAPTER 11

Powerfully Being Yourself.

* * *

Be Human.

Success in selling is all about standing out in today's sales environment. The modern sales consultant is human; he or she is someone that the customer can relate to, who is selling because he or she cares and wants to help. This is the key to success today. I often use examples such as "When I studied nutritional physiology…" and I add this fact in wherever suitable to show that I am a professional, that what I say is true, and that I actually care about health, although I have studied it for only half a year.

Customers like to learn something about you. It's important to show that you have a passion for what you're doing and that you have a relationship with what you're selling.

This makes you more human, helps you stand out, and makes you unique in the eyes of customers. You should also use stories that you have gathered about your product owing to natural interest and research to make yourself more relatable.

Share personal stories about yourself

Feel free to tell personal stories about yourself that customers can relate to. If customers mention a need, then tell them a story that they will empathize with. If you have been in their situations, tell them how you solved them. This will make you seem more human, and it'll be easier to sell the product.

Then go ahead with the sale.

Of course, you can also share stories about other people.

Identity Is the Most Powerful Driving Force in Behavior, Performance, and Results.

We can choose our own identities. Most people think it's impossible to create their own identities. They don't recognize how random their identities really are.

Who are you?.

Most people "are" who they've been told that they are. They "are" also what they've experienced. But this is not true.

We all have the power to be great salespeople, and our potentials are immeasurable. We are not our habits, our sports teams, our levels of positive traits, or our specific personalities. When we understand that, we can choose who we are and separate ourselves from our identities. We can choose to be whoever we want.

You do not "always show up to work on time," and you do not "always get the best results early" or "late in the day"—it's totally random. You act like the person you think you are.

For example, many sales consultants identify themselves as people who get ten sales, fifteen sales, thirty-five sales, and so forth per day, and this number affects them subconsciously in a significant way. The truth is that you can get massive number of sales every day. You are who you decide to be. If you currently make fifteen sales each day, aim to make your identity a twenty-sales-per-day person. Perhaps you should start thinking of yourself as a thirty-sales-a-day person, or an infinite-number-of-sales person. The greater your identity, the more sales you allow.

You should consciously be improving your identity or start with it being high. I saw myself as a fifty- or hundred-sales-a-day person, and I gradually made it all the way up, hitting a record of fifty sales in eight hours and fifteen minutes.

The identity I created for myself is that of a constantly optimal sales consultant. This is what I use as my guiding force. I like to be at my best, because it's much more fun that way. I am enthusiastic all day. While other people are at their peak enthusiasm levels for only a short period of time, I remain at my normal enthusiasm level all day. In addition, my habits are always working with me and have made it easier for me to be enthusiastic. This way you can make three to four times more sales than anyone else. This is because they don't have the same identity that you do.

Select and craft your own identity in a way that will enable you to perform optimally every day. We validate our identities every time we succeed, so keep it up.

Identity is the most powerful driving force in people. We go to extreme measures to continue being who we think we are (unless you are conscious of this and make adjustments). And remember who we "are" is totally random. Just imagine if the world were different. You would be completely different as well.

We can decide who we want to be, and the more beneficial our constructed identities are, the happier our lives will be.

Cristiano Ronaldo once said that he enjoyed working hard. He said, "It's part of me. I'm not doing this work because I have to. I'm doing it because it's a part of me."

Think about that statement for a second. When he was born, this work was not really part of him. This work is simply the identity he decided to create for himself because he thinks that he is *the best soccer player in the world*. No one is born with those kinds of thoughts. They are created. The mind-set of "Hard work is a part of me" and his other mind-set of "I am the best soccer player in the world" have both helped him become the world's best soccer player.

Take control of your own identity, and decide to be an identity that takes positive actions. As a result, you'll create a more positive life for yourself and others.

Imagine that you are a person with an even better sales average than you have today. Soon enough, you will be that person, as long as you keep evolving by learning and growing.

Who do you decide to be?

You Are in Charge.

You are the person in charge during a conversation. You are the leader. You lead the conversation. At the same time, you're also straightforward and want what's best for the customer. You're dominant and uplifting at the same time. You lift the customer up so that you can both be on the same level. You are not domineering; you are an inspirational leader.

Know the Success Factors and Dial Them In.

We need to dial in and add more enthusiasm, leadership, love, certainty, expertise, empathy, professionalism, humor, self-control, self-esteem, happiness, mirroring, chemistry, love of life, self-amusement, energy, fun, desire to help customers, determination, mission, and meaning.

There are more principles and qualities, but these are the most important qualities needed to be an appealing person. When you embody these qualities, customers will look up to you and often buy from you. The value you deliver is far beyond what they expect.

The more you embody all these principles, the more they will become part of you.

When you have the ability to dial in or adjust these qualities, you can consistently perform optimally.

You may already embody all or most of these principles on your best days. However, it's crucial that we balance these principles well so they complement instead of overshadow each other. Occasionally, we might need to remember to be empathetic while we're being especially dominant and enthusiastic. Other times, we may have good empathy and want what's best for our customers, but we aren't leading enough, so we dial up the leading.

The principles also impact each other. Empathy and leadership are connected. The more you lead, the more you will be respected by customers, and the more fun you will have as they show respect and openness.

The more you like yourself and do things in life that make you happy, the more you will like others, and the more they will like you. In other words, the more you like yourself, the easier it will be to show empathy. The more empathetic and helpful you are, the more you will like yourself, and the more you will lead.

Dial up different qualities and energies during sales conversations. The more enthusiastic you are, the more interest will be generated within the customer.

Sometimes when I sell, I envision an energy beam beaming from me to the customer. As the sale progresses, I imagine adding success factors that make the beam stronger and more centered. When you start to adjust the principles and energies rapidly, you can fine-tune the beam to send optimal energies as you wish.

When we are aware of all the success factors, understand why they are important, and understand how they increase buying temperature, we can be as great as we want to be.

You can also envision success factors as strings on a guitar that must be fine-tuned in order to perfect the sound, or as ingredients for a meal that the chef adds to balance the taste of a recipe. But I like to think of them as a beam of energy because this metaphor takes into account the force and energy output that I can put into various success factors, making my energy beam even clearer, stronger, and more focused on the customer. You can always love yourself and your life even more, be more genuinely empathetic, and so on. It's not enough to add just a tiny bit of empathy for success in selling. You have to have the right amount—and the more, the better. Customers love it, and it feels good.

You can always learn more about your product. You can always explain things in a more elegant way. You can always increase the power of the energy beam. The stronger the energy beam becomes, the better.

You must also take responsibility for increasing your own product knowledge so you can be even more creative in your sales conversations and gain more credibility. Some sales consultants think that they care a lot about customers, but they don't consider how much.

If you don't evaluate how much power you have within a sales principle, then how can you increase it?

Ask yourself these questions: How can I see the importance of my product even more? How can I feel what the benefits mean to those who receive this product? Why do I care for other people? What are the benefits of expressing empathy for the customer? Empathy is a great example of something that can be increased. If you learn to love your customers, you will create customers for life. You will also get great messages back from some of them who appreciated that you showed them kindness and compassion. It's great feeling to know that you had the power to contribute to the lives of others.

Imagine That You're Giving This Away for Free.

Your product has a good price, and you give more value to customers than they pay for.

With that said, one little trick I use is to imagine that I am giving them the product for free. Instead of selling, I'm simply making contact with customers to give them the product and tell them all the benefits they will receive. This way, I make my tonality even more confident and assuming of the sale, and I add words that are even more giving.

Of course, there is a price for everything, but your product is priced fairly, and they really are receiving your product as a gift from you.

I always end my conversations by saying, "You're welcome" and constantly remind myself that I'm *giving* each customer an improved life.

Toughness.

Toughness really consists of positivity and determination. When you are determined to be great, you become tough. Your positivity will shine through any challenges you might face, because different kinds of challenges might come, but those who win will always be those who overcome them and keep moving forward. The quality of toughness becomes ingrained in you when you respond to a challenge by smashing through it.

A challenge is merely a goal not yet realized. You simply want something, and then you get it—that's all. The challenges don't really matter, because you continue to realize your goals and dreams anyway.

Let's say, for example, that the calling system freezes because of a poor Internet connection or something. Since you are positive and were having a great conversation with the customer before the system froze, you'll just pick up your personal phone and call the customer back. You'll complete the sale while everyone else takes a break, which makes you a winner. Your toughness and positive outlook enable you to sell more than the others.

Sometimes it may not be possible to sell to a few customers because they have very serious reasons not to buy. In this case, you are satisfied since you did all you could. You continue to be in a peak state, and you are ready for the next conversation. You win by being this positive. As a result of your toughness and positivity, you may give your product to several people in a row in the following calls, just because you were ready for it.

Toughness is about always being optimistic and giving your full effort. You understand that the only thing that matters is your PMA and that you'll have a good day no matter what. This is why you're the best. Challenges are given to everyone (mostly due to lack of knowledge, which caused them), but if you are confronted by a challenge because you haven't proactively prepared, you'll crush it and earn many more sales than those who couldn't or wouldn't face and overcome their challenges.

It is a bit like Mario Kart or some other racing video game. There are occasionally banana peels or other obstacles in the way. If you're really skilled, you can avoid them. Sometimes, however, you aren't able to avoid them, but you keep a positive spirit and end up winning anyway.

Of course, some challenges are difficult to prepare for because we can't control everything in the world, and that's OK. But you are able to think deeply through how you can structure your life in a way that makes certain positive events inevitable. This goes very deep. The more success factors you are aware of, the more you are capable of shaping your life the way you want it. Thinking about all the ways you can make your success as inevitable as possible allows you to develop proactive responsibility. Think about this mind-set and how far it will take you in your success.

You can be smart and create a life with few challenges because you decide to eat healthy, get enough sleep, and be in top shape. But if you become sick, for example, despite all your best efforts, you can still go hard on your job and perform anyway.

Many of our challenges are similar to the challenges of others, and it's easy to see who tackles them in the best way. Sometimes we face challenges at different times than others, and whether we achieve good results during those challenging times will determine our success at the end of the month.

I still recommend that you think of the world as a positive place, where your work is fantastically fun and everything is going very well for you. You don't have to expect challenges; it's better to expect that everything will turn out great. By doing so, you will attract more positive things because by doing the right things, you will create more situations that are positive. This happens subconsciously. It's just that if challenges do come up, you power through them efficiently.

Thinking that the world is a positive place meant to help you grow is a principle. If you understand the purpose of this principle and apply it, you will increase your chances of creating great experiences in the future. Therefore, utilizing positive expectations is one of many ways to take proactive responsibility.

In fact, aside from some randomness, there are no challenges that cannot be overcome by being optimal and doing as much right as possible. This random world can be still be influenced by your conscious mind. Perhaps everything is happening within your own mind, and you can shape it the way you want, but there may be some elements of randomness even then. Nonetheless, keep on doing the right things, and your dreams, the goals you think about all the time, will manifest. You have got to give it your all.

Interpret everything as being positive. Imagine that everything is good, and justify why this situation is good in the same way that you interpret everything the customer says as something positive. Of course, if you do something that you know you shouldn't do, then you should connect a negative emotion to it and motivate yourself to change that behavior.

If you have done something that is not optimal, just decide to optimize your behavior in the future, and then focus on going to bed early, eating healthy, learning, being kind, working, and becoming a better person. Gradually everything that has happened to you will be positive because of some reasons you find for yourself.

SOME REASONS CAN INCLUDE THESE:.

- You learned valuable lessons.
- You are stronger.
- You are even more inspired.
- You learned how important it is to do the right things in life.
- If it hadn't happened, you wouldn't have learned [fill in the details].

You are tough. Things go well for you. The fact that you take optimal actions ensures that you proactively shape your life the best way possible and make sure you have the highest chances of great things happening in your life. Your highest goals are already fulfilled when you make the decision to be tough. Toughness is about staying in a positive mood, expecting positive events, and giving your all. Your life will be positive to the same degree that you are willing to make progress.

Michael Jordan said he interpreted everything that happened to him as something positive.

> *Sports is a tool that teaches. You know. It teaches you good things, it can also teach you bad things. It's how you perceive those things. I've looked at every experience I've had, both negative and positive, and taken that as a positive. I wouldn't change anything, because I think it would alter the other things that have happened.*
>
> —MICHAEL JORDAN

Look for the good, and you will always find it. Inevitably, you will become better in every way possible.

The tough person who gives it all he or she's got is optimistic and victorious because that person knows that a positive mind-set is the only thing that helps. He or she also knows that being optimistic improves creativity and that situations will only get better if one continues to learn and grow and become stronger. Life will always be better for the person who is tough and growing.

Caring.

Caring is one thing that cannot be emphasized enough when it comes to sales. Customers will notice that you enjoy helping people, and then they'll buy from you.

Being Just Good Enough to Close the Sale.

If you're just good enough to close one sale, then you're good enough to close a lot of sales. Small differences in skills can make a huge impact.

Imagine a high-jumper who makes it over a bar and can do so with a one-centimeter margin. Imagine the jumper jumping over that bar a hundred times; he or she probably wouldn't be successful every time. Then imagine that jumping over the bar represents closing a sale. If the height of the bar represents the required sales skills just to make a sale, imagine the difference it would make if he or she could jump ten centimeters higher. In other words, a little bit better equals a massive difference in the end. When you make the sale every time, you literally go from zero sales to one hundred.

You could also jump far over the bar, or jump over multiple bars (this means selling multiple products), if that's what you want.

It's all about just being great enough, and improving your ability to jump higher and higher, so that you have more and more clearing. Then even if very high bars show up, you can jump over them as well.

CHAPTER 12

Additional Tips and Strategies.

* * *

Race against the Clock.

This is a game you can play against yourself. Over time, you begin to know how many sales you should have at eleven o'clock, twelve thirty, two thirty, and so on. Set goals at these times, beat them, and then raise the goals in the future.

Compete with yourself. The better number you get by eleven o'clock, the closer you are to creating a great day. This will give you a great feeling of achievement as the day goes on, and you will also feel great about excelling in what you do. This will inspire you to give that extra effort to beat each subgoal throughout the day.

You will find that putting in more effort at the beginning of each period is a great way to stay ahead of your goals. Once you've reached and exceeded your first set of goals, you'll of course need to set higher ones.

You can always re-gear no matter what, but it's fun to compete with yourself, beat the clock, and focus on the next target.

For example:

I imagine I will have more than seven sales before eleven o'clock (so I'll envision having ten or eleven sales in my head). At ten o'clock, I'm already at five sales and have a great start. I get really pumped up, and then I end up with ten sales by eleven o'clock.

I feel great and aim at getting sixteen by twelve thirty. I end up achieving that goal too, and I immediately set a new goal for twenty-six by two thirty. I actually hit that goal, and I'm way ahead of the others, but I keep myself focused on the next goal.

I set a new goal to have thirty-five sales at four o'clock and beat that goal with thirty-six sales. By five o'clock, I predict I'll have at least forty or maybe even forty-five. I end up with forty-two sales at the end of the day, and that's a great result. This success was attained because I kept pushing myself and didn't settle when I reached my first goal. Instead, I increased the goal while visualizing myself progressing throughout the day. I had great periods every period because I set a fresh new goal every time. If I can acquire ten sales within the first two hours, I can surely beat that the next two hours, or at least make about ten sales during the next period as well.

This way of competing with yourself can create many fantastic, record-breaking days.

If you have four goal lines during the day, and you manage to get two additional sales during each time period, then you will end up with a total of eight additional sales per day. You will feel great and inspired, set good goals, and get well ahead of schedule, and it will work out in your favor. This is the power of setting subgoals and having checkpoints through the day.

Remember that the standard for what is possible can be increased too. I went from one-half of a sale per hour to seven sales per hour, and I have had periods where I managed to get ten sales per hour. These radical improvements helped me realize that we humans have a lot more going on than we think and that we're able to access this true potential if we are happy, decisive, and professional and if we mirror our customers, have fun, are enthusiastic about the benefits, and give away our products because our customers should obviously have them.

When are being your optimal self pretty much all the time and give it all you've got, not only will you improve drastically, but you'll find that optimal selling is easier and a lot more fun.

Be your best self when selling all the time. Some salespeople are optimal one hour of the day; you are optimal eight hours of the day. If you take the potential of your best-performing hour and multiply that by eight, you will know your true potential in selling.

Keep It Simple.

Keep everything you say so simple that the customer will understand every word. Customers want to hear only interesting things, and the things that are interesting to them are the things that benefit them.

Sure, people may be interested in how well you are doing or how something can benefit others, or they may simply find something fascinating. But for simplicity's sake, in sales, customers care only about benefits that will fulfill their needs. They just want to know what's in it for them, how much it costs, and how they can get their hands on it.

Of course, you need to show them how it works, why it works, and that you care about them and so on.

To keep things simple, refine your information, and select the most important things to say. Anything you say will either increase or decrease the buying temperature. If you keep your pitch nice and simple, that will also make the buyer think that the product is nice and simple to use. As you learn more and more about your product, you will have to mindfully refine and pick what's most important to share.

You can, of course, dig a little deeper into the topic to show your knowledge of the product if the customer also knows a bit about the topic. Some people love details, and others like efficiency, so tailor your presentations accordingly. But in general, keep it simple.

Working during the Silences.

The fastest way to beat the competition is by working when they're not working.

During peak working times, everyone makes progress to varying degrees.

There are moments during the day when everyone is in a peak state and going for it, and you can feel the work mode in the room. You can still get ahead by working smarter and more efficiently in those times and making progress faster than them.

However, during the day, there are also times that are more silent. These are times when your sales environment is calmer, usually right after lunch, during lunch, or some other period. Another silence might occur when people are watching TV. It could be at eight o'clock at night, when others do not utilize their time effectively. You know and can feel when those times are. This is a perfect time to read or listen to some sales training in your free time, because you know that you'll get back tenfold whatever effort you put in. Very few people are able to beat someone who *always* works on *what's most important*.

That's when you gain a lead on the competition. The others can't catch up to you if they're not running forward in life as fast or as consistently as you are. You'll have a *big* advantage if the others have paused and you continue running, or if you're in full sprint while they're just jogging. It is impossible for you not to win if you're running faster than the rest, and you're running while they're resting. Victory will then be inevitable. This is one principle Will Smith and Kobe Bryant ingrained as part of their identities.

Remember, though, that you are measuring only yourself against yourself. Your competition with others is just for fun. The purpose of the illustration above is to show clearly how powerful using the silences is. The only thing that matters is that you progress as much as possible. You actually want your competition to be as good as they can be, because they have their own goals that are different from yours. It's better for you that you both are living the life of your dreams rather than being stuck on who's better. The only way to achieve greatness is through collaboration with other people. There is no point in only being better than someone; the point is to become the best you can possibly be, and to get there, it helps to have great people around to grow with. Magically, when you help others, you will be lifted up yourself. You receive what you put out. If you help others grow, the universe will help you grow; trust that. Either way, it simply feels great to see people around you being happy and growing.

You will have personal silences, and as you become aware of them, you can begin to take advantage of them. One personal silence occurs when you are on your way to work. Spend your commute listening to sales training. If you listen to *Sales Greatness* or other sales training ten times with your headphones, the principles will effortlessly sink deeper and deeper into your subconscious mind.

If you use those silences, you'll be amazed at how much you can learn. When you listen to something productive while preparing food, cleaning, doing errands, shopping, driving, and so on, you will add one to two hours of additional learning time every day. Have that mp3 player, book, or phone ready, and learn every time you get a chance.

You also want to spend time thinking for yourself by writing down goals, ideas, and so on, but adding high-quality ideas to your brain is essential.

Many ideas will come from your listening to yourself. Through visualization and searching within, you can get ideas directly from the multiverse or mind, or wherever ideas come from. You are a genius, and you have special talents and visions.

When you want to consult the experience of others, don't ask just anyone. Spend time listening to the ideas of people who have already achieved the thing you desire to achieve. The ones you consult with or listen to should also live great lives. Some people can point you toward universal truths faster, but you have to be a good selector of whom you listen to. You must also select what is true among the knowledge they give you.

If you want to live a life filled with love, lots of money, freedom to do whatever you want, time to achieve things, fun, great achievements, and the ability to do anything you put your mind to, *charge into productive work in the silences.*

Try imagining your life as if you were completely happy. What does it look like when you realize your true reality and dream? How can you make that dream as great as possible? How can you make it even better?

During the silences, you create the magic in your life!

Eventually, you will enter a wave of continuous optimal actions. Sometimes the most optimal action can even be to meditate or lie on the beach talking to someone. Choose when you should sell, learn, train, think, and rest so that success becomes inevitable.

The easiest way to be constantly productive is to love what you do and sell something that you like to talk about.

I do *not* recommend working overtime in sales. It's better that you focus on optimizing sales per hour. Have fun, eat healthy, train, learn more about sales, increase your confidence, help the people around you, inspire yourself, and optimize all the things you do outside of work that will make you a truly great sales consultant.

Every Day Is a New Day.

The fun thing about sales is that every day is a new day. Every day we are given a new chance to set a record, learn more, and become better. Every day we get a new chance to optimize our sales abilities and have a fun day. You will love seeing how much progress you can make, the great results you can achieve, and how much passion and fun you can have.

SUMMARY.

* * *

I know that you will realize your true sales greatness.

Believe in yourself. Anything in the world can be learned. Sales can definitely be learned.

You can learn every aspect and detail of selling. As you do this, you will enjoy greater and greater success. Focus on the energies, and focus on the core principles.

The core principles need to be optimized. Optimize your product knowledge to the point where you are fascinated by your product and love it. Optimize your personality, and be your best self in your sales conversations. Be real and connect with customers. Care for customers, and help them in the best way possible.

Learn all the sales techniques you can and understand sales psychology, and use this knowledge while still being yourself.

Write down what works, and build upon that. Learn all the principles you need to learn, and optimize them.

Have fun. The more fun you have, the more productive you will be.

Help those around you.

I believe in you. All who decide to spend time learning about selling and their products eventually become great. How great you become depends upon how much you learn from optimal resources, how much knowledge you gather from inside yourself, and the degree to which you implement this knowledge.

Give your all, and you will be amazed by your own true sales greatness.

If you appreciate this book, I would greatly appreciate it if you gave a review and recommended this book to people you know who can benefit from it. You can follow this link to give a review:

https://www.amazon.com/review/create-review/ref=cm_cr_dp_no_rvw_e?ie=UTF8&asin=B01L07PKUG

Thank You!

*I wish you an optimal career in sales or whatever you do,
and I know you will bring value to a lot of people!*

Receive Optimal Tips!

* * *

In addition to all the information this book provides, there are a few tips I want to share with you via e-mail.

In these e mails, I will give you optimal tips in order to help you realize your sales greatness. They are aimed at optimizing your life as a whole.

Optimization consumes most of my time, and as a result, I constantly find new information that will help you become an even greater sales consultant. You will be informed about the very best success secrets I find along the way.

I spend a lot of time giving my friends advice, because I love it. So when you receive e-mails from me, I will give you the same advice that I give to my closest friends in sales.

These are some of the benefits you'll get from me:

- Sales tips
- Optimal success tips
- Inspiration
- The best sales programs in the world right now

- Great information I will come across in the future that I know will benefit you

To get this information, go to

www.SellingGreatness.com.

www.ingramcontent.com/pod-product-compliance
Lightning Source LLC
Chambersburg PA
CBHW070240190526
45169CB00001B/248